PICTURE HISTORY OF
WORLD WAR II
AMERICAN AIRCRAFT
PRODUCTION

Joshua Stoff

DOVER PUBLICATIONS, INC.
New York

Bibliographical Note

Picture History of World War II American Aircraft Production is
a new work, first published by Dover Publications, Inc., in 1993.

Edited by Alan Weissman
Designed by Jeanne Joudry

Library of Congress Cataloging-in-Publication Data

Stoff, Joshua.
  Picture history of World War II American aircraft production /
Joshua Stoff.
        p.   cm.
    Includes index.
    ISBN-13: 978-0-486-27618-2 (pbk.)
    ISBN-10: 0-486-27618-X (pbk.)
    1. Airplanes, Military—United States—Design and construc-
tion—History. 2. Airplanes, Military—United States—Design
and construction—Pictorial works. 3. World War, 1939-1945—
Aerial operations, American. I. Title. II. Title: Picture history of
World War Two American aircraft production.
TL685.3.S767 1993
623.7′46′097309044—dc20   93-15726
                                                                 CIP

Manufactured in the United States by LSC Communications
27618X08   2017
www.doverpublications.com

PREFACE

The photos in this book portray American aircraft production in World War II, including representative views of the various types of planes and operations involved. Lengthy research through various governmental and private archives failed to turn up production photos for all types of American World War II aircraft, and, of the production photos found, not all major operations in the construction process could be portrayed for each aircraft. Sadly, much has been lost to history. The photos presented here, however, do form a brief survey that conveys the massiveness of the American aircraft-production program and the speed and professionalism with which it was carried out. It is hoped that the reader will thereby come to appreciate what was done in those heady days of trial and tribulation of so long ago.

Special thanks to the following individuals and organizations for their support of this project: George Dade, Mike Machat, Jim Maas, Jay Frey, Peter Kirkup, Lois Lovisolo, Harry Gann and Jim Boss; the National Air and Space Museum, the Grumman Corporation, the McDonnell Douglas Corporation, the General Dynamics Corporation, the EDO Corporation and the Nassau County Museum.

JOSHUA STOFF

CONTENTS

INTRODUCTION

"The President talks of only 5,000 more planes and when I talk of
50,000 I'm called demented. But the time is going to come when
we'll be crying for 100,000 planes—and more."
—GENERAL WILLIAM ("BILLY") MITCHELL, 1936

One of the greatest industrial feats of all time was the massive production of aircraft by American manufacturers during World War II. In many ways, the Allied victory hinged on this huge American industrial contribution. This achievement also resulted in several new developments in American industry: (1) The true mass production of military aircraft, a phenomenon never seen before or since. (2) The unprecedented introduction of large numbers of women and minorities into the skilled work force. (3) The greatest period of camaraderie and high morale among workers—ever.

To a great extent the final victory in World War II was fashioned by the hands of millions of American aircraft workers. This miracle of mass production was created by workers who showed an extreme willingness to stay on the job—and not for money alone. They were certainly thankful for a good salary, but, realizing how heavily their son, husband, brother or fiancé relied on American production, they were determined not to let them lack for what they could make with their own hands. These millions of workers, only a few of whom were familiar with aircraft production before the war, formed the backbone of the aircraft industry. They learned new and repetitive jobs and did them for extended periods without complaint. These women and men are the unsung Americans who built with their own hands, rivet by rivet, each one of the over 300,000 military aircraft made in America during the Second World War.

The Depression left military aviation with little funding to purchase the number of aircraft desired in the 1930's. Only the steady drift toward war in Europe led to large production orders from overseas (as well as from America) and this forced a gradual buildup in production capacity. These foreign orders gave the American aviation industry a running start. Not until 1939 and the outbreak of war in Europe did military aviation begin to receive the governmental support it needed. Concerned by the possibility of war in Europe, President Roosevelt made a real commitment to air power in 1939 and pushed through a Congressional appropriation for 3,251 planes to be built within two years.

Furthermore, on May 16, 1940, prior to American entry into the war, President Roosevelt appeared before a joint session of Congress. Disturbed by the German invasion of Western Europe, Roosevelt demanded an immediate reappraisal of the American defense program. In an inspiring speech, the president noted the distinct possibility of attack by air. He then called for the American aircraft industry to turn out at least 50,000 planes a year. It was an astonishing request, but steps were immediately begun to implement it. After France fell in June 1940, Air Corps General Henry H.

("Hap") Arnold was told he would be given whatever funding he asked for. The job of building America's air armada had begun.

Achieving such massive production in such a short period of time, however, would prove to be an extremely difficult task. Existing aircraft factories would have to be greatly expanded and new factories built. Other manufacturers would have to learn how to build aircraft. Hundreds of thousands of new workers would have to be hired, most of them with no previous production experience. Massive subcontracting would also have to be initiated and many new production procedures developed. But it would take time to build the new plants. Skilled labor was hard to find and raw materials were scarce. Thus none of the new plants authorized in June 1940 had produced any aircraft by the time of the Japanese attack on Pearl Harbor. In spite of the many shortages and delays, however, new plants were eventually built and the old plants increased their production. Round-the-clock work shifts were also initiated. Thus the number of military aircraft produced rose from 402 in April 1940 to 2,464 in December 1941.

Then, the bombing of Pearl Harbor on December 7th of that year jolted America into an all-out production effort. It also united the nation as nothing else had before. President Roosevelt immediately gave the War Production Board the power to mobilize industry as needed. The Board quickly began to convert civilian industries to military production. The manufacture of automobiles was immediately stopped and the industry devoted all of its resources to aircraft (and other military) production. The labor unions also promised not to strike for the duration of the war; consequently there were few, if any, authorized job actions.

Nonetheless, if true mass production was to be achieved, a fundamental change in production methods was required. Production areas had to change from small flexible "job shops" to massive assembly lines. This radical change, however, would require a far greater degree of standardization of parts and processes than the industry had ever known. As aircraft were extremely complex products, this would prove to be a very difficult task. Thus the key to building large numbers of aircraft quickly was the introduction of the mass-production technique wherein large numbers of inexperienced workers were trained to perform simplified, repetitive tasks.

As there was only a fairly small demand for military aircraft prior to 1941, aircraft at that time could be virtually handmade. Because many of the parts of these planes were "handmade"—mass-production jigs and fixtures were not then in use—they were usually not interchangeable, and additional work was required in the assembly area to make them fit. They often had to be filed or forced to fit onto the aircraft.

These pre-1941 military aircraft were also built on a lot basis, as orders were so small. Production machinery would turn out only the limited number of parts required and then be put to another use. There was virtually no such thing as an assembly line; rather, complete aircraft were built entirely in one spot on the factory floor. Thus these prewar aircraft factories could be termed "job shops." Their layout was small and flexible, and they could handle a variety of projects at once, but such shops were fit only for low-volume production.

American aircraft manufacturers realized they had to increase their output drastically; thus they turned to assembly-line techniques, in which the unfinished aircraft would be moved through different areas, with progressively laid-out work operations. The introduction of the aircraft assembly line was the first great step needed to achieve mass production. Now aircraft could move from start to finish without stopping or backtracking. Thus most plants built during the war were designed as long, skinny buildings to accommodate these new assembly lines. In order to keep the assembly lines moving, feeder and subassembly lines were established so that the correct numbers of parts and subassemblies were turned out to keep the final-assembly line flowing. The move toward mass production also brought with it standardization, this despite the necessity for constantly upgrading military aircraft based on combat experience. Ultimately the Air Corps was forced to set up 28 modification centers just to retrofit brand-new planes based on the latest combat intelligence.

As auto makers would now be building aircraft, the American automobile industry was sure its already established mass-production methods could work wonders, but, to its embarrassment, it discovered that aircraft were far more difficult to produce than it had imagined, being more complex than cars and requiring closer tolerances.

Because of their inherent complexity, designing and producing World War II aircraft was a difficult job, calling for a greater degree of specialization. Thus aircraft production was divided among different companies that produced airframes, engines, instruments, propellers, landing gear and many other specialized subassemblies and components. A primary contractor would assemble these components into a complete aircraft and was thus relieved of much of the design and manufacturing work for the subassemblies.

Constructing airframes occupied the bulk of World War II aircraft production. An airframe is the load-carrying structure of the aircraft and includes the wings, the tail, the fuselage, the control surfaces and the metal skin that covers all of these parts. In 1940 many more companies were producing airframes than engines, there being 13 major airframe plants managed by 11 different companies. During the war 16 new branch airframe plants were constructed and they produced over 30 percent of the aircraft built. During the war, however, only four major airframe plants were run by companies who had not been producing aircraft prior to 1940. Nonetheless, by 1944, the Ford plant at Willow Run produced more airframe poundage than any other aircraft plant.

Airframes were made of structural components known as spars, stringers, bulkheads, ribs and frames, with an outside covering called the skin. The airframe and skin were usually aluminum, although some parts were made from aluminum

or steel forgings, castings or extrusions. The number of parts contained in these airframes was tremendous. For instance, a B-25 airframe consisted of 165,000 parts, held together by over 150,000 rivets. All this did *not* include the parts contained in the engines, propellers, instruments and yet other smaller parts! In contrast, a modern automobile contains about 4,000 parts.

In 1940 there were but three major American producers of aircraft engines for military use. The biggest were Pratt & Whitney and Wright Aeronautical (the other was Allison). Both of these were established companies that were now expanding as a result of foreign orders. In mid-1940, however, when it became clear that the number of engines needed would exceed their production capacity, it was decided to supplement this production by bringing automobile-engine makers into the aircraft-production fold. Thus Pratt & Whitney licensed the R-2800 to Ford in August 1940, and the R-1830 to Buick in October. At the same time they expanded their East Hartford plant. Ultimately between 1940 and 1944 almost half of the total engine production was by these new licensee plants. In 1944 they delivered 60 percent of the engines, even though prior to Pearl Harbor not a single one had produced an aircraft engine.

These engines also required a very high standard of quality of manufacture. For example, the R-2800 had 13,000 parts, 1,400 of them different types and almost all of them moving or in contact with moving parts. This necessitated a high degree of finishing and very close tolerances. This in turn meant a great number of both operations and inspections. To produce a connecting rod alone required 90 operations with 100 inspections. Such precision also led to a large number of rejections following an instrumented test run. These rejections meant that all the time spent on their manufacture had been wasted.

Because of the massive demand for aircraft, in 1942 competition was ended between aircraft manufacturers, and true teamwork began. Each company then shared with all the other companies all the production knowledge it had gathered over the years. The manufacturing knowledge of each company became the common property of the industry. This was the first—and last—time the aircraft-production industry was unified. In fact, by mid-1943 many companies were making aircraft designed by a former rival. Not only Boeing built B-17's, but so did Douglas and Vega (Lockheed). Both Brewster and Goodyear began to turn out Vought Corsairs. Associated industries also produced complete aircraft, such as Ford at Willow Run, which turned out B-24's. Even a house builder on Long Island (Dade Brothers, Inc., of Mineola) turned to the manufacture of Waco CG-4 troop gliders. By the end of 1942, near-miracles in mass production were occurring. Factories were converted and new factories built, and huge numbers of planes rolled off the assembly lines without end.

The level of aircraft production soon reached an amazing magnitude. Starting in early 1942, factories ran 24 hours a day, seven days a week. Some workers spent as many as 80 hours a week on the job. Women, who generally performed simplified, repetitive tasks under the supervision of experienced prewar male workers, eventually made up 40 percent of the work force and helped expand the total aircraft-industry labor force to an astonishing 2.1 million by the end of 1943.

Beginning in 1942 there was a remarkable rise in both the efficiency of production and the spirit of cooperation among thousands of formerly rival firms. As the need for competition was eliminated, cooperation among all prime contractors, subcontractors and licensee firms soared. Clearly the wartime demand for aircraft was far beyond the ability of any one firm's capacity to produce them. Between 1942 and 1944 the aircraft industry's production increased tenfold. American aviation was unquestionably the greatest single industry in the world, and this may well have been the greatest single factor in winning World War II, a performance that rates undoubtedly as one of the greatest production feats of all time.

In 1943 aircraft production stood at 7,172 planes per month. By 1944 it was an amazing 9,000. Owing to new production efficiency, these 1944 planes also cost about 40 percent less than the same planes two years earlier. For example in March 1942 B-24's cost $238,000 each. In March 1944 they cost $137,000. The number of man-hours needed to build a B-17 also fell from 55,000 to 19,000. By mid-1944, 15 airframe builders were turning out 23 different types of combat aircraft.

These massive increases in production meant that even a major manufacturer could no longer build a complete aircraft. Thus during 1943 the concept of mass subcontracting was introduced. Factories best able to do a particular job did a growing share of the industry's work in making that product. Much of this work was done by smaller companies that, after hesitating at first, rapidly expanded their production lines. In essence they became departments of the prime contractors.

The first company to introduce mass subcontracting was Lockheed early in 1943. Faced with greatly increasing orders for P-38's, Lockheed was unable to meet the demand in-house. Their Burbank plant was already working at capacity, and expansion would take too long. Thus Lockheed began to contract with many smaller manufacturers to produce subassemblies for P-38's. Lockheed's main Burbank plant then turned into an assembly plant more than a true manufacturing plant. After the "Lockheed Plan" was successfully implemented, most other airframe contractors followed suit. This last step finally put the American aviation industry on a true mass-production basis.

Throughout the war, there was also a continual effort within each plant to simplify all production techniques and machinery. In other efforts to increase production, various prizes and war bonds were offered for efficiency, and suggestion boxes were placed throughout the plants.

Clearly, the smashing defeat of the Axis powers was the result not only of the skill and courage of American aviators but equally of the patriotic hard work of American aircraft workers, who provided such an overwhelming number of aircraft. Finding these workers, however, in the huge numbers needed, was the aircraft industry's greatest problem during the war. Thus every manufacturer made a major effort to attract and hold new workers. There was a complete morale-building effort within each company through music, sports and lunch-hour entertainment. Returning war heroes would also visit the factories that built their aircraft, one of the best ways of increasing the employees' satisfaction with their jobs. Activities such as these created welcome breaks in workers' routines, because most performed tasks that were repetitive by nature. Run on a national basis, these programs were successful, and they helped create a high level of camaraderie and morale among workers that has never been equaled. The incentive of fairly high wages, too, increased the number of workers in the industry; there was also, however, an obvious patriotic dedication among both labor

and management that facilitated the completion of the huge task facing them.

In 1939 there were only 48,638 aircraft workers in the United States. However, by November 1943, the industry had managed to hire and train an astounding 2,102,000. Amassing this titanic work force required every known technique of personnel recruiting and the creation of several new ones. Retired workers were asked to return, women were urged to leave their homes (with on-site day care available), and everyone from gas-station attendants to businessmen worked on night shifts while also keeping their regular daytime jobs. Teenagers often worked after school and during summer vacations. Drives to reduce absenteeism were also instituted. Also, in a radical break with the past, minorities were actively recruited into the work force. Where before they had met with discrimination, now they were met with open arms.

Perhaps the most noteworthy labor achievement of the war was the mass introduction of women into the work force. With the women came the necessity of making great changes in factory life. Women personnel counselors were hired, separate rest and recreational facilities were created, and day-care nurseries for their children were set up on-site. The newly hired women planemakers proved completely capable in nearly all jobs and veritably superior to men in certain operations. These included tedious jobs that demanded long hours of continuous work of a repetitious nature. Not surprisingly, many women's hands also proved to be more disposed toward the finer work of aircraft construction. By mid-1944 almost 40 percent of the airframe workers were women, and their patience and skill proved remarkable. Ultimately, the efficiency of women, in terms of yield vs. hours, also proved to be above that of male workers.

In all, during the war, and while increasing production, the industry produced a total of 150 separate types of aircraft, and of these there were 417 different models. This achievement is remarkable in that it generally took three years to design, develop and produce a new military aircraft. In 1940 there were 41 airframe and engine plants; by 1943 there were 86. From January 1, 1940, to August 14, 1945, the U.S. spent $45 billion on aircraft. In return a total of 300,317 military aircraft were produced. This was enough to equip 16,680 squadrons, or one airplane for every 434 Americans. The Army Air Force accepted 188,880 planes including 61,221 bombers and 57,050 fighters. The major bombers produced were B-29's (3,760), B-24's (18,188) and B-17's (12,677). The most heavily produced Air Corps fighters were the P-47 (15,485), the P-51 (14,501) and the P-40 (13,700). The C-47 was the most heavily produced transport (10,245). Monthly production soared from 2,464 planes in December 1940 to a high of 9,113 planes in March 1944. This massive number of aircraft was needed, as the life expectancy of a heavy bomber in the 8th Air Force was approximately 45 missions (about eight months). Peak Air Corps inventory was 89,000 planes in July 1944. Occasionally some outdated planes, such as the Curtiss P-40, were kept in production until superior types were more widely available. It is also extraordinary to note how few "lemons," such as the Brewster "Buccaneer," got into production. Many big gambles paid off greatly, such as the huge orders for 1,644 B-29's and 777 P-47's before even the first one flew.

Not unexpectedly, with victory on V-J Day (August 15, 1945), contracts for an additional 31,000 aircraft were cancelled. This amounted to 95 percent of all military contracts. The immediate effect of these cancellations was the complete layoff of well over one million workers, the closing of plants, and the beginning of the scrapping of this vast armada. P-47's and B-17's would have little use in peacetime America.

The principal role played by American air power in winning World War II, however, is a fact widely accepted by all sides. This air power was clearly dependent upon the rapid expansion of production achieved by the aircraft industry, the result of the sweat, determination and hard work of millions of American men and women. After the war's end, German Field Marshal Albert Kesselring stated: "Allied air power was the biggest single reason for Germany's defeat."

Here, then, is how we built that air power, a phenomenon never seen again. This book is for the millions of nameless, unsung American heroes who helped achieve victory with rivet guns and welding torches. . . .

Production Processes

1. Some of the processes used in fabricating aircraft are shown in this and the following six photos. Here, rolling aluminum sheet for aircraft skin at the Alcoa plant. *(Photo: Cradle of Aviation Museum, Mitchel Field, L.I., N.Y.)*

2. Welding an engine mount in a jig, using electric arc welding. *(Photo: Cradle of Aviation Museum.)*

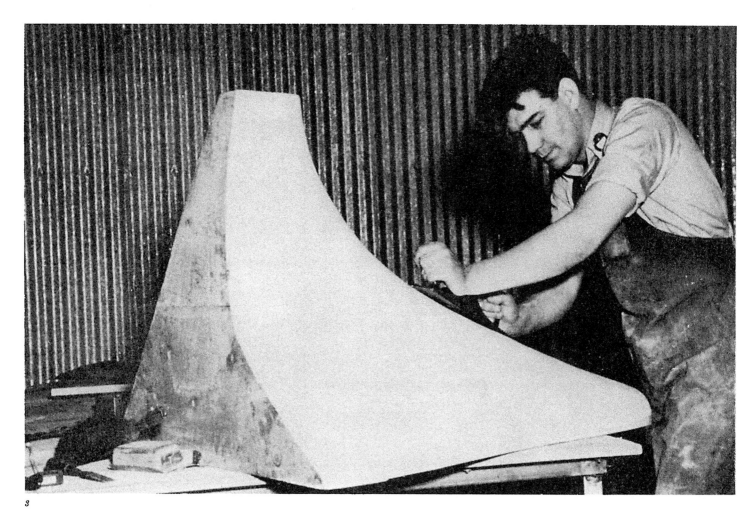

3

3. Shaping wood to be used as a mold for pressing skin sections. *(Photo: Cradle of Aviation Museum.)*

4. Pressing an aluminum nose cowl in a mold for a Piper L-4. *(Photo: Cradle of Aviation Museum.)*

5. Spray-painting doors for a Bell P-39 in the paint shop (note the lack of masks). *(Photo: Cradle of Aviation Museum.)*

6. Anodizing aluminum parts in a chemical tank. Anodizing parts prevented corrosion. *(Photo: Cradle of Aviation Museum.)*

7. Riveting the skin on an aircraft's wing. The worker on top is using a compressed-air rivet gun to hammer the rivet; the worker on the bottom has a bucking bar to flatten out the rivet end, holding the riveted parts tightly together. *(Photo: Cradle of Aviation Museum.)*

4

5

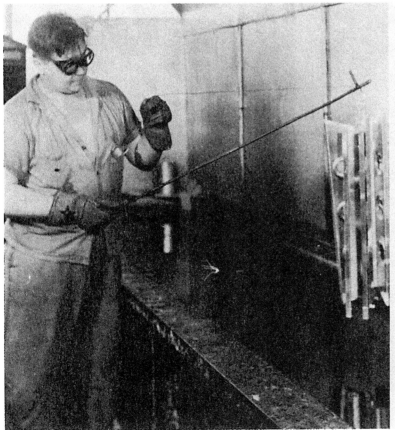

6

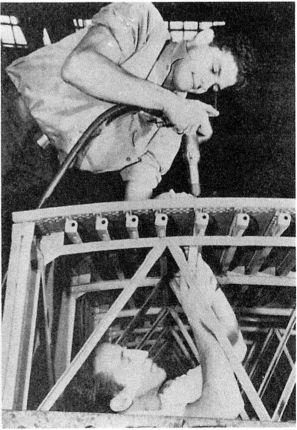

7

Prewar Production

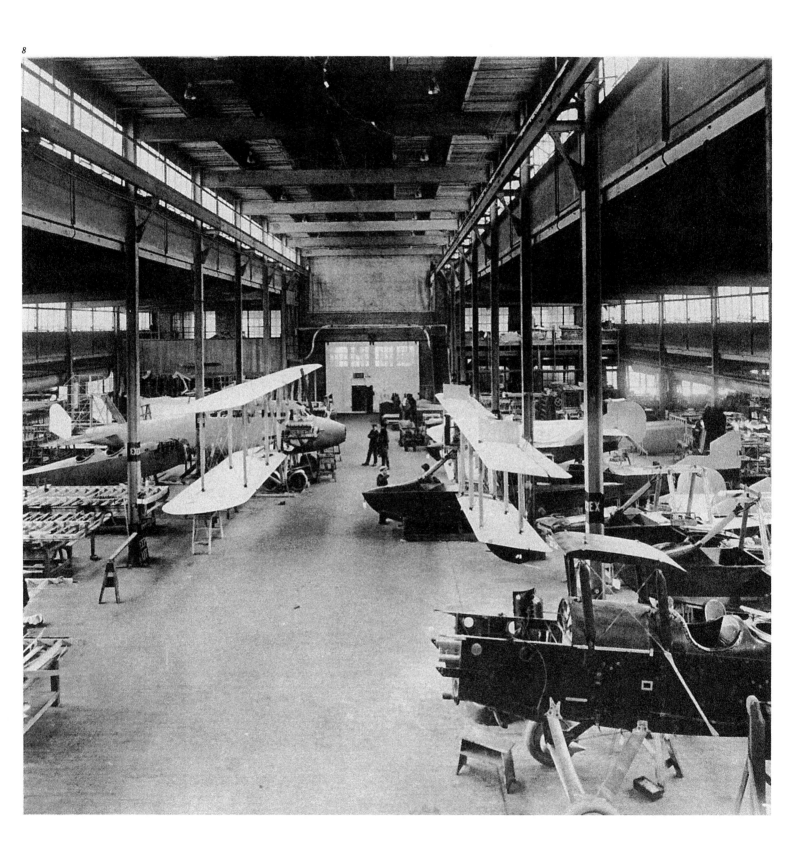

8. A classic example of prewar aircraft production, at the Curtiss factory, Garden City, New York, circa 1920. Note the great number of obstructions within the building—obviously not designed for mass production. Also note four different types of aircraft under construction all in one large area. The Curtiss plant was clearly a "job shop": small, flexible and able to handle a wide variety of projects at once, but fit only for low-volume production. *(Photo: Cradle of Aviation Museum.)*

9. The small number of military aircraft procured prior to the Second World War meant that these aircraft were "handmade" in small lots. Here, craftsmen assemble Martin bomber engine nacelles, Cleveland, 1922. Such handmade parts were fitted to a particular aircraft and were usually not interchangeable with parts from other planes of the same type. Note the lack of jigs, fixtures, power tools . . . and women. *(Photo: Cradle of Aviation Museum.)*

9

10

11

10. Before 1941, when military aircraft were built on a lot basis, only a limited number of parts were made and then the machinery was put to another use. As this photo of a Consolidated P2Y flying boat under construction in Buffalo, in 1928, also reveals, there was virtually no assembly line. Rather, complete aircraft were built almost entirely in one spot on the floor. If mass production was to be achieved, obviously fundamental changes in production methods were required. *(Photo: Cradle of Aviation Museum.)*

11. Realizing they would have to increase their out-

put drastically, manufacturers turned to assembly-line techniques. Prewar assembly lines were small and inefficient, however. The assembly line for Seversky BT-8 trainers in Farmingdale, New York, in 1934 shows the limited extent of prewar military production. In one short line the entire aircraft went from a basic framework (on the right in the photo) to completion (on the left). Most subassemblies were built right in front of the aircraft! The introduction of efficient assembly lines would be the first step needed to achieve true mass production. *(Photo: Cradle of Aviation Museum.)*

Fuselage Construction

12

12. For some years from its inception in 1932, the Brewster Aeronautical Corporation remained a relatively small organization. Not until 1939 did the work force exceed 1,000. With the start of production of their first fighter, the F2A "Buffalo," in 1940, the work force soared to 7,000. This was Brewster's first, and most famous, production aircraft, first ordered in 1936. It had a Wright R-1820 engine, hydraulically retractable landing gear, and all-metal stressed-skin flush-riveted construction. It was assured its place in history as the U.S. Navy's first operational monoplane fighter. Brewster President James Work clung to the idea that an urban aircraft factory was possible. This belief resulted in an inadequate, inefficient plant in Long Island City, New York. Brewster set up shop in the old seven-story Ford building, thus resulting in the only vertical aircraft factory in the world. By necessity, aircraft under construction had to be maneuvered around posts and up and down the only elevator in the building. Brewster's cramped conditions at its Long Island City plant are plainly evident in this 1939 photo, as this Buffalo fuselage receives its skin. *(Photo: Jim Maas.)*

13. The Curtiss P-40 "Warhawk," developed from the P-36, was America's foremost fighter in service when World War II began. P-40's engaged Japanese aircraft during the attack on Pearl Harbor and the invasion of the Philippines in December 1941. They were also flown in China by the famed Flying Tigers in 1942. Historically the P-40 is one of the more controversial American fighters of World War II. Clearly it was inferior to most German and Japanese fighters, yet the fact remains that in the dark days following Pearl Harbor America had only one fighter plane in quantity production—the Curtiss P-40. The P-40 fuselage was of full monocoque construction built in upper and lower halves joined along the horizontal centerline. The forward half of the fuselage consisted of the pilot's quarters and his controls and instruments. The rear half housed the baggage compartment, accessory equipment and tail gear. These P-40E fuselages in Curtiss' Buffalo, New York, plant, in 1941, await their engine mounts and cockpit equipment before moving onto the final assembly line. *(Photo: National Air and Space Museum, Washington, D.C.)*

13

14

14. The Curtiss C-46 "Commando," widely used in the Pacific Theater during World War II, was the largest and heaviest twin-engine plane in operational use by the Army Air Corps. The plane originated in a 1937 design for a 36-passenger luxury airliner, the prototype of which was built in St. Louis in 1940. Army interest was aroused by this new airliner because of its especially large fuselage. A contract was placed for 46 units of a military version, designated C-46. In May 1942, the first C-46 was rolled out of the Curtiss factory in Buffalo. The C-46 was designed to be pressurized for substratosphere flying, which resulted in a sturdy and unusual fuselage design. The C-46 fuselage shown in this 1942 photo is just beginning to get its skin attached. The vertical bulkheads are connected by horizontal stringers. *(Photo: National Art and Space Museum.)*

15. As it was to be pressurized, the C-46 fuselage was rather interesting. In cross section it was formed of two intersecting circles with the common chord of intersection being the cabin floor line. A circular section was decided upon because it was ideal for pressurization. However, one circle for the size of airplane involved would have presented excessive frontal area that would have greatly reduced aerodynamic efficiency. But by using two circles, frontal area was reduced without losing the ideal pressure section, and the common chord line served the dual purpose of tying the circles together and providing the floor structure. Flush riveting was used in the drag-sensitive areas of the fuselage. These workers complete the fuselage center section prior to attachment of the nose. *(Photo: National Air and Space Museum.)*

15

16. With the successful introduction of the Curtiss C-46 into service with the Air Transport Command and Troop Carrier Command in 1942, coupled with the pressing need to provide the U.S. Army with airlift capability, orders for the C-46 mounted rapidly. The C-46A had a large cargo door in the rear fuselage and folding seats along the cabin walls for 40 troops. From this photo it is obvious how the windshield was designed to follow the contour of the fuselage to increase performance. The fuselage nose was also readily removable to facilitate inspection and service of plumbing and wiring in back of the instrument panel. *(Photo: National Air and Space Museum.)*

17. The fuselage of the C-46 provided approximately 2,300 cubic feet of cargo space. The floor, adjacent to the cargo door in this photo, was practically level (the main portion of floor was but 9.5 degrees from horizontal) to expedite loading and unloading when the aircraft was on the ground. Evident here are rows of metal tubes running the full length of the compartment, which were intended to protect the fuselage walls from damage by cargo. *(Photo: National Air and Space Museum.)*

17

16

18

18. The Naval aircraft that took the brunt of the fighting in the early part of World War II, while superior aircraft were still taking shape, was the Grumman F4F "Wildcat." Once the war began in Europe, isolationism was perceived to be a dangerous course for the U.S. Thus, while in 1939 the Navy had placed orders for just 78 of the original F4F Wildcats, total F4F orders for 1940 amounted to 759. Here Wildcat fuselages are taking shape at Grumman's Bethpage, New York, Plant 2, in 1941. Plant 2 was the first plant erected at Government expense for a defense contractor under the Emergency Plant Facilities Act. These F4F's will be receiving their engines in the next station. Wing- and tail-surface attachment will follow. *(Photo: Grumman Aerospace Corp.)*

19. The Grumman F4F retained the distinctive blunt appearance that characterized earlier Grumman fighters. The single fixed wing was mounted squarely on the fuselage centerline, and the retractable landing gear was operated by a handcrank. The Wildcat was powered by a 1,050-hp Pratt & Whitney R-1830 engine. More than any other U.S. aircraft manufacturer, Grumman was to concentrate its wartime effort at one site, Bethpage, building aircraft chiefly for one customer—the U.S. Navy. This F4F has had its engine mated, and internal connections are now being made. The windscreen has already been masked for painting. *(Photo: Grumman Corporation, Bethpage, N.Y.)*

19

20

22

20. The Grumman F6F "Hellcat" started out as a modification of the F4F Wildcat—larger, faster and greatly improved—in 1942. As the design developed, however, it turned out to be a very different airplane, now powered by the 2,000-hp Pratt & Whitney R-2800 engine. The main problem with the Hellcat, though, was not the needed modifications, but rather how to get it into production fast enough. The first Grumman Hellcats were built on a preproduction line at Grumman's Bethpage works, while a new plant dedicated solely to F6F production was being constructed in 1942. To avoid delay while the Navy acquired the necessary priorities for the issue of steel for the new plant, Grumman's President, "Jake" Swirbul, bought steel beams as scrap from New York's old Second Avenue elevated railway and assembled them into Plant 3 (also in Bethpage). The first production jigs were erected in October, and F6F's started moving down the assembly line before the plant itself had been finished. Here, Hellcat fuselages take shape in Plant 3. Wing stubs and tail surfaces will be attached next. *(Photo: Grumman Corporation.)*

21. The first Grumman F6F was built in August 1942; in five months the F6F productivity curve had sprung upward, and they began to roll off the assembly line. This was unheard-of speed in an industry that used to need years to move from blueprints to planes. One full Hellcat squadron was ready and delivered by December. The Hellcat was the only U.S. fighter ever that from the first example required no developmental work before it could successfully engage in combat. Here, a work force mostly of women rivets the skin on Hellcat fuselage aft sections. As Grumman needed thousands of new workers to build their Hellcats, they were among the first companies to hire large numbers of black workers, drawing on nearby Long Island and New York communities. *(Photo: Grumman Corporation.)*

22. A worker at Grumman rivets the skin on a Hellcat fuselage aft section. Another worker on the inside will flatten the rivet with a bucking bar. Unriveted skin sections are held on by temporary fasteners, which can be seen sticking out. Grumman's F6F was all-metal except for fabric covering on the control surfaces. The semimonocoque fuselage had vertical keels on each side of the centerline with aluminum sheet frames, aligned by stringers, riveted to them. The aluminum alloy skin was made up of lateral strips flush-riveted on the outer surface. The low midwing had folding outer panels attached to the wing stubs. These wings folded back in the same fashion as the later Wildcat wings and reduced the wingspan from 42 to 16 feet. *(Photo: Grumman Corporation.)*

23

25

24

23. A fat-bodied midwing monoplane, the TBF "Avenger" had typical Grumman lines, its most noticeable feature being its very deep fuselage, which enabled a torpedo or bombs to be totally enclosed. A typically sturdy Grumman all-metal aircraft, the TBF was one of the biggest and heaviest aircraft ever designed for carrier operation up until this time. The original TBF was unveiled on December 7, 1941, just as the Japanese were attacking Pearl Harbor. In light of Japanese actions that day the plane was named the "Avenger." Here work is progressing on a TBF's forward fuselage, with the skin just being riveted on. The bulkhead-and-stringer construction is plainly visible inside. *(Photo: Grumman Corporation.)*

24. The Grumman TBF had a crew of three, an internal bomb bay and a power-operated turret. The landing gear retracted into the wings, which folded back for carrier stowage. The Avenger's pilot released the torpedo and the gunner's turret was provided with a .50-caliber machine gun. An additional gun was in the plane's belly. This TBF forward fuselage is receiving its aluminum skin by an all-woman production team. By the end of 1943 more than 5,000 Grumman

employees had gone into military service. They were replaced almost entirely by women to keep the production lines rolling. Grumman's work force peaked at 25,500 in September 1943. The "Grumman Aircraft" coveralls were optional and cost employees $2.50 each. *(Photo: Grumman Corporation.)*

25. The Bell P-39 "Airacobra" was one of America's first-line pursuit planes in December 1941. By the time of the Pearl Harbor attack almost 600 had been built at Bell's Buffalo, New York, plant. The most unusual feature of the P-39 was that the engine was located in the center of the fuselage, behind the pilot. The fuselage of the P-39 comprised two spliced sections known as the "forward" and "aft" fuselages. The entirety of the forward fuselage was built around a heavy automobile-like chassis, seen here under construction. This chassis supported the engine, propeller, cockpit, wing center section, nosegear and all accessories. Because of its multipurpose usage, the chassis was built up of two longitudinal beams that were cradle shape in profile. Each beam was made of extruded aluminum alloy tied together with heavily reinforced aluminum webbing. *(Photo: National Air and Space Museum.)*

26

27

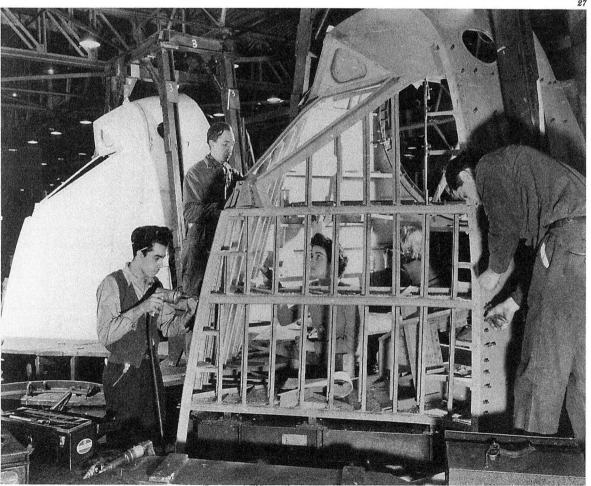

26. Ideally, the best place for an aircraft's engine is right at its center of gravity. This allows for a streamlined nose and excellent maneuverability, but it also presents the problem of delivering the power to a propeller on the aircraft's nose. In the case of the P-39, the propeller was driven by an eight-foot extension shaft passing under the cockpit to a gearbox in the nose. The pilot's cabin was superimposed on the forward part of the fuselage chassis and attached as an integral part of the fuselage. The Allison V-1710 engine was located on the chassis bed to the rear of the cabin. Air to cool the engine was taken in by scoops in the fuselage sides. The forward and aft fuselage sections, visible here, have been joined by nuts and bolts through stiffeners and bulkheads just aft of the engine compartment. The outer skin, made of formed aluminum sheet, is being riveted to the fuselage bulkheads. *(Photo: National Air and Space Museum.)*

27. The Martin PBM "Mariner" was the most widely used American flying boat of World War II. It was intended as a U.S. Navy long-range antisubmarine patrol-bomber and air-sea rescue aircraft. In this 1943 photo, Mariner nose sections are under construction. Of conventional rib-and-stringer construction, the skin can be seen being riveted on the right half of the structure. The cutout on the left is for the turret mounting two .50-caliber machine guns. *(Photo: National Air and Space Museum.)*

28. PBM Mariner fuselages under construction at the Martin plant near Baltimore. The Mariner was the largest twin-engine flying boat ever built. Its fuselage (hull) was an all-metal semimonocoque two-step structure with alclad covering (see Glossary). Once the basic PBM hull was completed, it was moved via an overhead rail to the final assembly area. When war broke out in 1939 there were only 3,900 employees on the Martin payroll, but by the end of 1940 there were 13,000. By Christmas 1942 the total had reached 53,000. *(Photo: National Air and Space Museum.)*

28

29

30

31

32

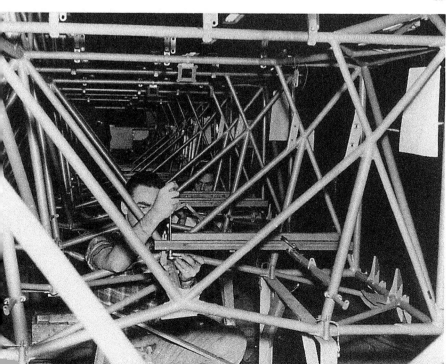

33

29. The Beech Aircraft Company of Wichita, Kansas, was a prewar maker of private and small-transport aircraft. In 1940, the Air Corps ordered 150 bomber versions of their Beech 18 transport for use as bomber trainers. Changes included a transparent nose, bomb bay, internal bomb racks and provisions for flexible guns for gunnery training. There were several orders for the plane, which became the Army AT-11 bombing and gunnery trainer. More than 90 percent of the Air Force's 45,000 bombardiers were to learn their skills in the AT-11 during the war. Student bombardiers normally dropped 100-lb sand-filled practice bombs. Ultimately 1,582 AT-11's were built at a cost of $67,000 each. Here, seemingly endless rows of shiny AT-11 fuselages are nearing completion at the Beech plant. (Photo: National Air and Space Museum.)

30. The North American B-25 "Mitchell" was the most heavily produced twin-engine American bomber of World War II. This improvement on earlier North Amrican designs was built primarily at North American's Inglewood, California, plant and first flew in 1940. The B-25 fuselage center section shown in this 1942 photo is ready to receive the rear section, engines and landing gear. The front and center sections of the fuselage, including the wing center section and engine nacelles, have been joined. The aircraft is leaving the powered portion of North American's overhead tramrail and is being rolled by hand onto a turntable. (Photo: Cradle of Aviation Museum.)

31. The B-25 fuselage center section reached from the nose to the end of the bomb bay. It was built integrally with the wing center section and consisted of a series of four longerons, frames and stringers. The roof of the bomb bay served as the floor of a crawlway to permit crew travel fore and aft. The wing center section had two main spars to resist bending loads and six ribs to distribute landing loads. From the turntable, this fuselage is heading off to the place where the tail section will be joined to it. (Photo: Cradle of Aviation Museum.)

32. This B-25 rear-fuselage assembly line flows toward the turntable of the center-fuselage-section assembly line, at a right angle to that line. The two fuselage sections will be joined where the two lines meet. Note the engine-preparation line paralleling the rear-fuselage assembly line. The rear fuselage section, reaching from the bomb bay to the tail, had four longerons connected to the center section as well as many stringers and formers. B-25's were built at North American's Inglewood plant until 1944, when the plant was turned over to P-51 production. A second B-25 plant was established near Kansas City, and Mitchells were built there until the end of the war. (Photo: Cradle of Aviation Museum.)

33. The North American AT-6 evolved out of a design competition authorized by the Army Air Corps in 1937 to develop a Basic Combat Trainer. This was a new category of aircraft that incorporated the equipment and characteristics of an operational combat plane. In effect it was a combat-ready plane used as a trainer. Because it was a trainer it had to be of very robust construction. Thus most of the fuselage had an inner skeleton of heavy welded steel, seen here under construction. (Photo: National Air and Space Museum.)

34

35

36

34. This 1943 view of the main assembly area for AT-6's, at North American's Inglewood, California, plant, shows many trainers in various stages of construction. The aft fuselage was of all-metal monocoque construction while the forward half consisted of welded steel-tube framing with removable side panels, as seen on the right. North American set new records for production at the time by delivering 60 airplanes in August and another 60 in September 1938. By early 1939 there were six different models of the AT-6 in production. Accelerated pilot training in the U.S. due to the onset of the war led to an immediate surge of orders for the AT-6A. The Air Corps placed a contract for over 500 AT-6A's in 1941 and the Navy ordered practically the same plane, the SNJ-3. The main difference between the AT-6 and SNJ-3 was that in the SNJ-3's the airframe and all the hardware were zinc-chromated to protect against salt-air corrosion. By the end of 1941 a new contract for 1,032 AT-6's was awarded to North American to be built at its new Dallas, Texas, plant. *(Photo: Cradle of Aviation Museum.)*

35. The North American P-51 "Mustang" was designed in 1940 at the request of the British, who badly needed new figher aircraft. Built at North American's Inglewood, California, and Dallas, Texas, plants, early versions of the P-51 were powered by Allison V-1710 engines. U.S. Army Air Corps purchases of the Allison-powered Mustangs began in 1941, primarily for photo-reconnaissance and ground-support use because of its limited high-altitude performance. However, the British modified one aircraft with a Rolls-Royce Merlin engine, and, as a result of this testing, the Air Corps ordered 2,200 more of this version before even the first American one had flown. The Merlin-powered version had a much improved speed and service ceiling. The Mustang's fuselage was an aluminum alloy monocoque structure built in three main sections. The motor-mount section, the center section and the tail unit all bolted together. In this 1943 photo the skin is being riveted on a P-51B fuselage center section at the Inglewood plant. *(Photo: National Air and Space Museum.)*

36. Assembled P-51B fuselages being worked on at North American's Inglewood plant. The cockpit area, visible as the cutout in the fuselage, contained steel armor both fore and aft. The fuselage center section weighed 1,100 pounds, the nose section 2,250 pounds and the tail unit just 150 pounds. The main intake for the engine was below and aft of the fuselage's center, a place that was found by wind-tunnel testing to create less drag. The Merlin-powered P-51B and its Dallas-built twin, the P-51C, began operations in December 1943. *(Photo: National Air and Space Museum.)*

37

37. The Lockheed P-38 "Lightning" was an all-metal long-range midwing fighter. First designed in 1937 as a high-altitude interceptor, it was the first American twin-engine fighter. Lockheed's P-38 assembly line at Burbank was over 820 feet long, creating an efficient straight-line flow from raw material through the fabrication process and on into final assembly. From the first mating jig till the nearly complete aircraft reached the hangar door there were 30 separate assembly stations. The fabricated parts were delivered to the component-assembly sections at the beginning of the 820-foot line. Upon completion of the wing center section, it progressed to a station where the forward booms and the fuselage were attached. Parallel with the main-boom and center-section assembly operations were the assembly operations for the forward booms and the fuselage, the assembly of these components terminating at the mating station. On the right can be seen one of the two booms that extended aft from the engine nacelles to support the tail unit. Air scoops, seen on the outboard sides of the booms, provided air for the induction system, going to the coolant radiators and superchargers. *(Photo: National Air and Space Museum.)*

38. This 1944 scene at Lockheed's Burbank plant shows a P-38's fuselage, center section and tail boom being assembled. The design featured twin all-metal, flush-riveted tail booms of aluminum alloy construction with stressed-skin covering. P-38's were of semi-monocoque construction for great strength, with considerable stainless steel being used in the boom areas around the superchargers. The central nacelle (fuselage) was an all-metal stressed-skin structure accommodating the pilot, nose gear and armament. It extended forward from the trailing edge of the center section. *(Photo: National Air and Space Museum.)*

39. Lighter-than-air (airship) operations were also successfully employed by the Navy during World War II. Two-hundred-fifty-foot-long K-type airships were used for coastal and antisubmarine patrol. With a 2,500-mile range they could stay aloft for up to 50 hours. Able to travel low and slow, they could detect submarines as deep as 90 feet, and then hover over and bomb them. No vessels were sunk by enemy submarines while escorted by airships. This scene shows the world's first, and only, airship control-car mass-production line at the Goodyear plant, Akron, Ohio. Eight men rode in the all-aluminum control car, which also supported two engines on outriggers. The open top area of the control car was mated to the inflated gas envelope. *(Photo: Goodyear Aerospace Corp.)*

38

39

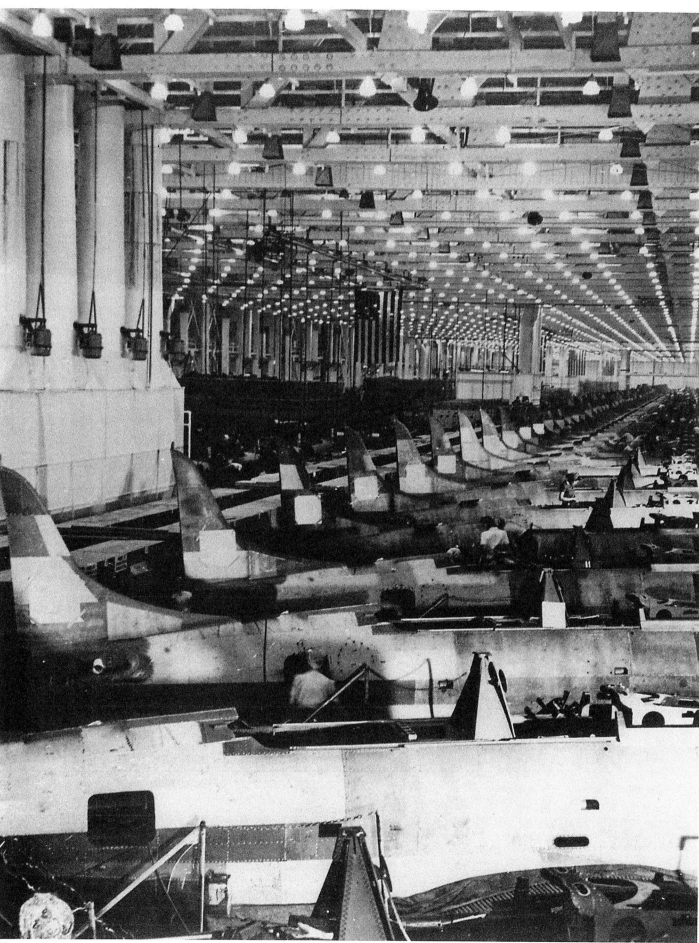

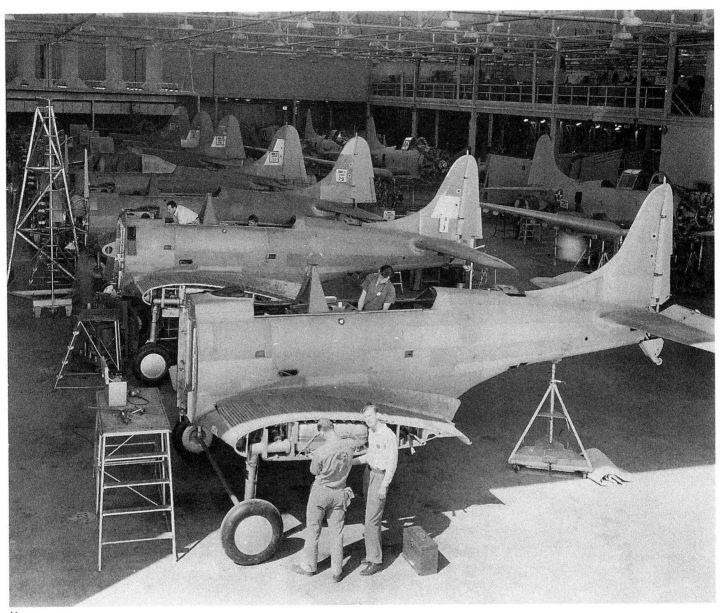

41

40. For the greater part of World War II, the principal Navy dive bomber was the Douglas SBD "Dauntless," a refinement of the 1935 Northrop BT-1. Although probably obsolescent by the time of Pearl Harbor, Douglas received continuing orders for the SBD, as there was no real replacement. This scene of SBD production at Douglas' El Segundo, California, plant shows SBD fuselages still in an early stage of assembly. Tail surfaces, wing stubs and engine have still not been mated. *(Photo: National Air and Space Museum.)*

41. The Douglas SBD was an all-metal low-wing carrier-based dive bomber. Most SBD's had two .50-caliber guns in the cowling and two flexible .30-caliber guns in the rear cockpit. Self-sealing fuel tanks were first introduced on the SBD-3. Most models were equipped with 1,000-hp Wright R-1820 engines. Here, at the El Segundo plant, the wing stubs and all tail surfaces have been attached. The wheels having been built into the wing stubs, the aircraft can now be moved on its own gear. In this 1942 photo, the cockpit interior is being fitted and the canopy attached. *(Photo: McDonnell Douglas Corp.)*

42

42. No airplane used by the Army Air Forces was used more widely or for so long as the Douglas C-47 "Skytrain" transport. It was produced in greater numbers than any other Army transport and was used in every combat theater of World War II. The C-47 was developed from the Douglas DC-3 airliner, which first flew in 1935. The Army, eager to buy the C-47 cargo version of the DC-3, asked Douglas to make only a few changes: a stronger cabin floor, large cargo doors and more powerful engines. Here C-47 fuselages are nearing completion at Douglas' new Long Beach, California, plant. Engines and outer wing panels have yet to be attached. *(Photo: National Air and Space Museum.)*

43. The C-47 was of all-metal semimonocoque design with smooth-riveted skin. The airframe was covered with alclad aluminum, highly resistant to corrosion. At this stage of the C-47 assembly line in Long Beach, in 1944, the interiors are being fitted out and the rudders and elevators are going on. Note the clock (upper right) indicating the next time the whole assembly line will move ahead. The large cargo door is plainly evident. This door had to be large enough to fit a jeep or cannon through, and the floor and rear fuselage were reinforced to hold the heavy cargo. The C-47 could carry up to 27 troops. *(Photo: McDonnell Douglas Corp.)*

44. The Republic P-47 "Thunderbolt" was the biggest, heaviest and most rugged American fighter to see combat during World War II, a great improvement over earlier Republic/Seversky fighter designs. Impressed with the P-47's design statistics, in September 1940 the Air Corps issued a whopping $56-million-dollar contract to Republic for 171 P-47B's and 602 P-47C's—all ordered before the first one had flown. This was the largest single order for fighter aircraft placed up to that time by the Air Corps. The fuselage of the P-47 was of semimonocoque, all-metal construction, composed of transverse bulkheads and longitudinal stringers. The main forward part of the fuselage was built in two units, top and bottom, bolted together. Seen here, workers in Republic's Farmingdale, Long Island, New York, plant, in 1943, are drilling and riveting the bulkheads to the longerons in the upper section of the fuselage. The hoses carry compressed air to power hand tools. *(Photo: Cradle of Aviation Museum.)*

43

44

45

45. Upon completion of the framework of the P-47 fuselage, both halves were covered with alclad sheeting, flush-riveted. The pins seen sticking out of the framework of these upper halves are "cleco clips," devices that held the skin in place while it was being riveted on. There were over 79,000 rivets in a P-47. These fuselages are for early "D"-model "razorback" Thunderbolts. *(Photo: Cradle of Aviation Museum.)*

46. Late 1940 was furious and frantic for Republic (as for the world in general). By the end of the year employment at Republic reached 2,600, up from just

176 in 1939, and the factory expanded greatly in order to meet growing contract obligations. Within one year the entire company had expanded to the point where it was second only to the much older Curtiss company as the largest supplier of Air Corps fighters. Here, at Republic's Long Island plant, P-47D upper-fuselage frames (on the left) are being covered with aluminum skin (shown finished on the right). Engines will then be added and the fuselages will move on to the final assembly area at the rear. P-47's were first delivered to the Air Corps in 1942, and they began to see combat in the spring of 1943. *(Photo: Cradle of Aviation Museum.)*

46

47. Upon completion of the P-47 main fuselage halves they were bolted together along the centerline, as seen here. The lower half had additional reinforcing around the wing-hinge fittings. The front stainless-steel firewall bulkhead can also be seen. The P-47 was unique in many respects. Its supercharging system, at its heart, created many problems during the design stage. In order to enable the aircraft to attain 400 mph, maintaining a smooth airflow between the supercharger and the engine was the most serious design consideration. Consequently, the supercharging system was designed first, in order to obtain the most efficient and least interrupted airflow, and the rest of the aircraft was designed around it. The supercharger was placed in the fuselage aft of the pilot, with exhaust gases piped back to the turbine and expelled at the rear; ducted air was returned to the engine under pressure. Despite the fact that the supercharger was in the tail and the engine in the nose, the system proved quite successful. *(Photo: Cradle of Aviation Museum.)*

47

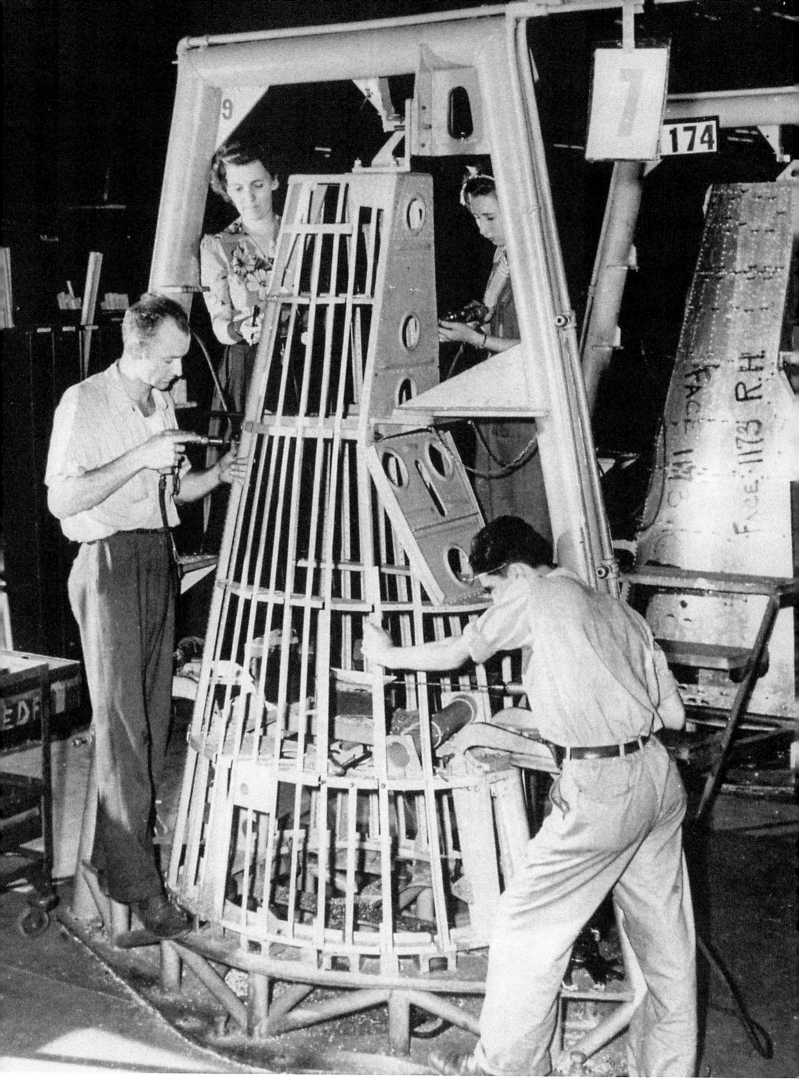

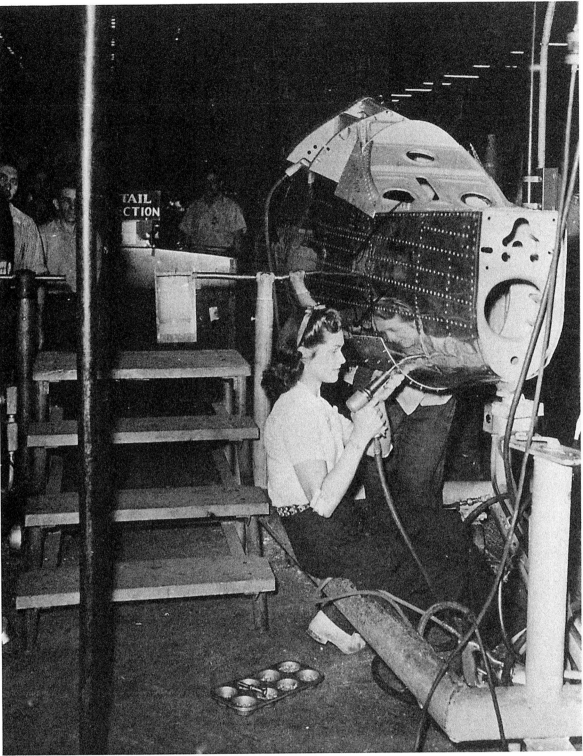

49

48. The P-47 fuselage aft section was constructed as one complete unit and then attached to the forward sections. As can be seen here in the vertical jig in which it was assembled, it was built, much like the forward half, of a series of frames tied by stringers. The tailwheel frame was especially reinforced to absorb landing loads. The cutout in the upper right portion of the section is where the fin and stabilizer were attached. The tail section standing at the right in the photo is already covered with skin. *(Photo: Cradle of Aviation Museum.)*

49. Upon completion, P-47 tail sections were riveted and bolted to the last frame of the main fuselage. The alclad skin was also brought forward and riveted to the same place. This worker, sitting on the fuselage jig, is using a compressed-air rivet gun in the tailwheel area of the aft fuselage. A tray with plenty of rivets lies at her feet. *(Photo: Cradle of Aviation Museum.)*

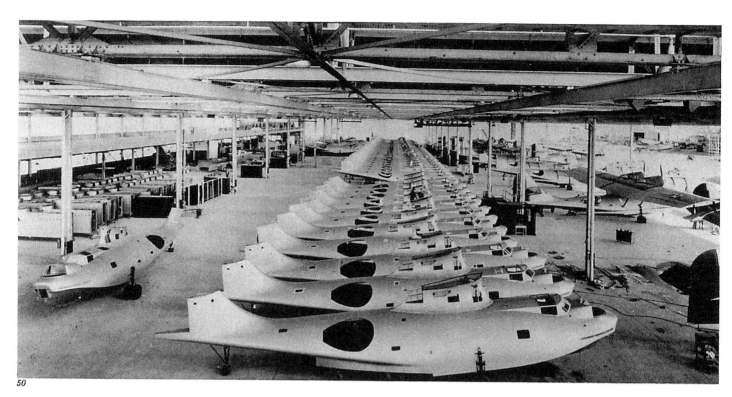

50

51

6-22-36

52

50. The Consolidated PBY "Catalina" was one of the world's first all-metal flying boats, the most successful flying boat operated by U.S. forces in World War II and the most heavily produced flying boat of all time. Built in Consolidated's San Diego factory, the PBY was designed as a long-range patrol bomber, as it was able to carry a substantial bomb load. The hull, seen here under construction in 1942, was of monocoque design, consisting of bulkheads and stringers divided into watertight compartments equipped with watertight doors. Its aluminum alloy skin was flush-riveted. The PBY saw extensive use by the allies in all theaters. When America entered the war in December 1941, the Catalina was the principal patrol bomber in service with the U.S. Navy, and it played a prominent part in operations in the Pacific area right from the start. PBY's played crucial roles as reconnaissance aircraft in the battles of Midway and the Aleutians. PBY's also rescued downed pilots, conducted long-range reconnaissance missions and sank enemy submarines. Consolidated built a total of 2,398 Catalinas in both flying-boat and amphibious versions. *(Photo: National Air and Space Museum.)*

51. These prewar PBY fuselages (in a photo dated June 22, 1936) nearing completion clearly show the two-step hull design. Badly needing more workers,

Consolidated in San Diego set up training schools wherever it could, in old storerooms, schools and buildings left over from the San Diego Exposition. Thousands of workers went to these schools, most of them having never before been in a factory. Consolidated also concentrated on trying to hire local workers rather than outside people, since there was already a severe housing shortage in the San Diego area. The cutout in the nose of each fuselage in this photo is for a machine-gun turret. One .30-caliber gun was also placed in each waist blister. *(Photo: National Air and Space Museum.)*

52. More Consolidated B-24's were deployed during World War II than any other type of four-engine bomber. Massive formations of B-24's were used on long-range bombing missions in all theaters during the war. This view shows the early stage of fuselage construction at Ford's huge Willow Run plant in Michigan. Nose sections are being assembled on the right, aft sections on the left, and subassemblies for the nose in the middle. According to wartime statistics, one B-24 used enough aluminum for 55,000 coffee percolators, enough alloy steel for 6,800 irons, enough steel for 160 washing machines, enough rubber for 800 automobile tires and enough copper for 500 radios. *(Photo: Cradle of Aviation Museum.)*

53

53. The original Consolidated plant for B-24's was located in San Diego. The Consolidated Aircraft Corporation, having only recently moved from Buffalo to San Diego, was ripe for building the Army's second heavy bomber (after the B-17). Peak employment at the San Diego plant was 45,000, 40 percent women. Subcontractors often employed up to 90 percent women. The nearly completed B-24 nose-section subassemblies seen here will now be moved by overhead conveyor to the final assembly area, where a Plexiglas framework will be added to cover the opening in the nose. *(Photo: National Air and Space Museum.)*

54. The aft sections of the B-24 fuselage taking shape at Consolidated's Fort Worth, Texas, plant, in 1943. The B-24's frame-and-stringer construction can be seen at the lower left, with the aluminum skin being riveted on at the lower right. Once completed, the aft sections were moved via overhead crane to the final assembly area, as seen here. Note the cutout in the tail for the tail turret, and the crane operator who moves along with the fuselage on the overhead rail. *(Photo: General Dynamics Corp.)*

54

55. Northrop's large twin-engined P-61 "Black Widow" was the first American fighter designed specifically as a night interceptor. Before the first one was ready to fly, the Air Corps ordered 560. The Black Widow carried three crewmen and four 20mm cannons under the cockpit canopy. Here a P-61 crew nacelle takes shape at Northrop's Hawthorne, California, plant. The crew nacelle was a semimonocoque, flush-riveted structure. The wing's front and rear spars were bolted to spar extensions that passed through the center of the nacelle in front of and behind the gun turret. The gun turret was mounted between these spars and protruded through the top of the crew nacelle. Note the arrangement around the nacelle of platforms for the workers. *(Photo: National Air and Space Museum.)*

56. At the heart of the P-61 night fighter was its radar equipment, enclosed in the nose section. This section, constructed of resin-impregnated fiberglass, was attached to the crew nacelle by four locating studs and four toggle latches. While the plane's interceptor equipment was working, an antenna in the nose section, consisting of a reflector with a slender arm projecting from its center, whirled constantly, emitting radar waves. Any waves that encountered an obstacle in the form of another aircraft were bounced back to the radar antenna, alerting the crew to the possibility that the enemy was near. The P-61 was a tricycle gear plane, clearly indicated by the nosewheel visible here, in this 1944 photo. *(Photo: National Air and Space Museum.)*

57. The most widely used U.S. troop/cargo glider of World War II was the Waco CG-4A. The sturdy but simple fuselage of this troop glider was made of welded steel tubing with a wooden floor and wooden nose. All of this was then fabric-covered. Although able to carry a heavy load, gliders offered little protection from groundfire, and they were not considered desirable duty. The box-section fuselages had an upward-hinged nose section to permit direct loading and unloading of troops and vehicles into and out of the cabin. The hinged portion of the nose had a towline attachment and contained the cockpit with dual control for two pilots side-by-side. Each glider cost $24,000. They were generally considered expendable in combat and were abandoned or destroyed after landing. Here, at the General Aircraft plant in Queens, New York, in 1944, these nearly completed glider fuselages await their fabric covering. *(Photo: Cradle of Aviation Museum.)*

58. Workers at the Ford plant in Michigan sew the fabric covering on the center section of a CG-4 glider fuselage. The fabric will then be doped and painted olive drab. The welded-steel-tubing fuselage is open on the bottom so the wooden floor can form the fourth side. Gliders went into operation in July 1943 during the Allied invasion of Sicily. They also successfully participated in the D-Day assault on France on June 6, 1944, and in other important airborne operations in Europe and the Far East. *(Photo: Cradle of Aviation Museum.)*

58

57

59

59. In 1934, Boeing of Seattle was invited to participate in an Army competition for a new multiengine bomber. Their model 299 was conceived for a purely defensive mission: the protection of the American coastline from foreign surface fleets. It was this function, and not the formidable defensive armament, that led to the famous name "Flying Fortress." The first YIB-17 (the prototype) was flown in 1936. Ultimately, however, the B-17 became one of the best-known and most widely used bombers of World War II. In the center sections shown here, the skeleton of the semi-monocoque fuselage of the B-17 was formed by a series of big aluminum-alloy rings tied together with aluminum strips. The rings that gave the fuselage its circular shape were called circumferential stiffeners.

Their outer edge was flanged to form a surface to which the aluminum skin was attached. The inner edge was notched with V-shaped slots. Aluminum strips, called longitudinal stiffeners, fitted into the slots and tied the circumferentials together to form the skeleton of the fuselage. Each piece of the sheet-metal covering, or "skin," was pierced with little aluminum tubes. The little tubes clipped the aluminum sheets to each point where circumferential and longitudinal stiffeners crossed one another, holding the sheets in place until they were riveted to the fuselage. When rivets were driven in they passed right through the holes in the tubes, virtually melting them into the aluminum skin of the plane. *(Photo: National Air and Space Museum.)*

60

60. The Boeing B-17 fuselage was built in four sections: the forward section, the center section, the rear half, and the "stinger" tail section. Each section was built in its own frame (jig). The skeleton of the fuselage was assembled first and made rigid, the bulkheads that separated the section from the others were installed, then the section was covered with its skin of sheet aluminum. Once this was done it was moved in its carrying cradle to the forward production line, close to the final-assembly area. Here each section was completed. Radios were installed, all instruments, wiring assemblies, the seats, controls and a multitude of other items were fitted. Wires to other sections were also fitted for rapid connecting. When the sections of the B-17 were completed, such as this already-combined forward and center section, they were moved into position on their carrying cradle or overhead crane (as seen in this 1944 photo) and joined to make the completed fuselage. *(Photo: National Air and Space Museum.)*

61. A B-17 in its final form took up a lot of space. To eliminate this problem and to speed up production, Boeing production engineers devised a plan whereby the Flying Fortress could be completed in sections, then assembled just before it was ready to roll out the factory door. This system was called "multiline" production. The multiline system reversed the usual aircraft production process of assembling a plane in its final form at the earliest possible moment in manufacturing. Under the older assembly-line system workers performed thousands of interior installations after the ship was assembled in its final form. This meant that in

a plane as large as the B-17 large numbers of workers would have had to enter and leave the ship by its few doors. The multiline system eliminated this loss of time and effort by using a series of short lines. Each of these short lines built one section of the plane. These sections were called "pre-completes." The B-17E forward fuselage pre-completes seen here will be mated with the aft fuselages at the next station. Maximum B-17 production at Boeing was reached in April 1944 when 16 B-17G's per day were being rolled out. *(Photo: National Air and Space Museum.)*

62. If for no other reason than the part it played in bringing an early end to World War II, the Boeing B-29 "Superfortress" must be recognized as one of the great planes in the history of aviation. It was also the subject of a massive development program that in four years designed, built and tested one of the most complex pieces of movable machinery ever made until that time. The B-29 was designed in 1940 as a replacement for the B-17 and B-24. When the XB-29 first flew in September 1942, it was far ahead of its contemporaries. The ten-gun defensive armament was concentrated in four remote-controlled power turrets on the fuselage and a single directly controlled turret in the tail. The crew-occupied areas of the fuselage were divided into three pressurized compartments to increase crew efficiency and comfort during long high-altitude missions: one in the nose for the pilots, bombardier and flight engineer; one amidships for the gunners and observers (seen here under construction); and a separate pressurized area for the tail gunner. *(Photo: National Air and Space Museum.)*

61

62

63

63. Even before the prototype was completed, the Air Corps ordered the B-29 into large-scale production. The Boeing Wichita Division was expanded for the purpose and the Renton and Seattle Number 2 plants converted to B-29 production. Bell and Martin were also ordered to build B-29's in new plants to be constructed at Marietta, Georgia, and Omaha, Nebraska. B-29 production became the largest single airplane program of World War II. It entailed not only a multiplant production complex and thousands of subcontractors, but also modification centers where last-minute changes and refinements could be made without slowing the expanding assembly lines. While manned turrets were considered for the B-29, they were rejected as unsuitable for the operating altitudes envisioned, and instead a remote-control system with gunners operating the turrets from five sighting stations in the pressurized areas of the plane was used. Full pressurization of the fuselage was considered impractical in a bomber, so only the crew areas were pressurized. The nose and mid-fuselage sections were connected by a tunnel through the bomb bays that allowed crew members to change positions during pressurized flight. The tunnel is visible in this 1945 photo at the top center of each fuselage center section. *(Photo: National Air and Space Museum.)*

64. Rushed into combat without the normal testing program, the Boeing B-29 was initially not a good aircraft. As a major step forward in technology, the B-29 had problems all its own. Furthermore, it was used in conjunction with the all-new 2,200-hp Wright R-3350 engine, a nearly impossible challenge to operate. After many modifications, however, the B-29 became a very good aircraft. In addition to incorporating many "firsts," such as pressurization and remote-control power turrets, the B-29 was the world's heaviest production airplane as a result of the increases in range, bomb-load and defensive requirements made by the Army. The Superfortress was in fact the first military aircraft of any type to be pressurized. This allowed the crewmen to move about freely in the plane's interior, breathing normal heated air at high altitudes. It also eliminated the need for individual oxygen supplies and electric flying suits. Here a B-29 pressurized nose section is being assembled in a large fixture. The opening for the pressurized tunnel at its rear can be seen at the top of the fuselage. *(Photo: National Air and Space Museum.)*

65

65. The 18-foot nose section of a B-29 contained 50,000 rivets and 8,000 kinds of parts obtained from over 1,500 subcontractors. There were also eight miles of electrical wiring in the aircraft. The skin seams on the pressurized sections of the B-29 had to be both riveted and sealed with a tape impregnated with a compound and inserted into the joints before riveting. All rivets, even repair rivets, had to be dipped in sealing compound before installation. Since control cables passed through pressurized sections, synthetic-rubber bushings gripped the cable hard enough to stop air leakage.

Pressurized construction also allowed for an unusual degree of soundproofing and cabin heating. The B-29 fuselage was lined with a sound-deadening and insulating blanket made of equal parts of animal hair, cotton and kapok (because of a shortage of kapok, fiberglass was soon substituted). These inch-thick blankets made the B-29 World War II's quietest bomber. Seen here are B-29 nose sections under construction on a moving-rail system at Boeing's Renton plant. *(Photo: National Air and Space Museum.)*

Wing Construction

66. Constructing a P-47 wing trailing-edge section in Republic's Farmingdale plant. The P-47 wing was a full cantilever type employing two main spars supporting the attachment of wing to fuselage. There were also three secondary spars, one each for supporting aileron, flap and undercarriage assemblies. The wing's flush-riveted, stressed-skin surface was reinforced by extruded angle stringers. The ailerons were also metal-covered. *(Photo: Cradle of Aviation Museum.)*

66

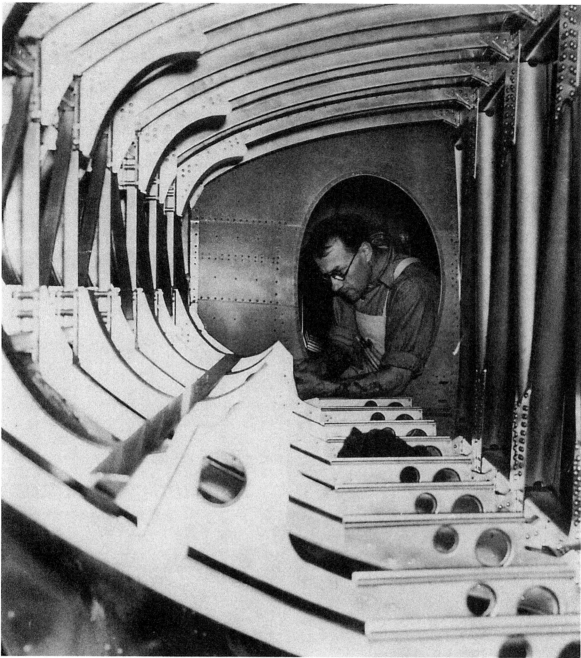

67

67. This worker is doing some detail work inside the wing of the famous Boeing B-17. The long spars on the right, forming the main support of the wings, were built of aluminum-alloy beams trussed by aluminum tubes and riveted together into a solid structure. This type of construction, though comparatively light, produced a spar of great strength with an ability to stand a strain many times the weight demanded of it, as well as to absorb gunfire without crippling the plane. The spars were tied together with ribs placed at intervals along the entire length of the wing. The ribs, curved to form the shape of the wing, were constructed of aluminum beams reinforced by aluminum bars trussed together by aluminum plates and rivets. *(Photo: National Air and Space Museum.)*

68. The B-17's two wings were built as one piece of five sections. The center section was incorporated in the forward half of the fuselage. The remainder of each wing was composed of an inboard section, with the engines, and an outboard section. When each section was completed it was moved by overhead crane to the installation line, where it was completed with engines and cowling, gas lines, flaps, ailerons, landing gear, bullet-proof fuel tanks, de-icer boots, wires, lights and other essentials. Here, inboard wing panels of a Flying Fortress are about to be mated with the fuselage. *(Photo: National Air and Space Museum.)*

69. Inboard B-17 wing panels take shape at Boeing's Number 2 plant in Seattle. Each wing panel of the Flying Fortress was made as a unit in the construction jig with engine nacelles included. From the leading edge back about two-thirds of the way to the trailing edge the skin was reinforced with corrugated aluminum-alloy sheet riveted to the ribs. From there on back the skin was attached to built-up aluminum-alloy ribs. *(Photo: Cradle of Aviation Museum.)*

70. Because of its unorthodox twin-engine, twin-boom design, the Lockheed P-38 experienced growing pains and required several years to perfect. Superior speed, rapid climb, high ceiling and great firepower were the principal Army objectives in the design. The main center-section spar was the first subassembly in Lockheed's Burbank, California, assembly line. At the station shown here, the main spars are being assembled, with ribs and various other details, into complete center wing sections. *(Photo: Cradle of Aviation Museum.)*

71

71. Eventually 16 companies manufactured 13,906 Waco CG-4 troop gliders during World War II, including Ford, 4,190; Northwestern, 1,510; Commonwealth, 1,470; General Aircraft, 1,112; and Waco, 1,075. The CG-4A was constructed of fabric-covered wood and metal and could carry 15 troops or a jeep or cannon. It was towed aloft by either a C-46 or C-47. Originally a house-building and trucking company in the prewar years, Dade Brothers of Mineola, New York, constructed the wooden wings to match the fuselages built by nearby General Aircraft of Queens, New York. This photo shows the spruce truss ribs that made up the leading edge of one wing. *(Photo: George Dade.)*

72. The wide chord of the wing of a CG-4 glider is clearly evident in this photo at the Dade Brothers glider plant. Each spruce rib was made up of three separate sections and its trusswork was glued and nailed together. The cutout for the aileron can be seen at the top. Remarkably, women made up almost 90 percent of the work force at the Dade plant. *(Photo: George Dade.)*

73. When the assembly of the spars and ribs was complete, each wing, of two panels each, was covered with thin mahogany plywood. The completed wings were then shipped from Dade Brothers to General Aircraft, where they were covered with cotton fabric, doped and painted olive drab. *(Photo: George Dade.)*

73

74

74. The Vought F4U "Corsair," built in Stratford, Connecticut, was the fastest Naval fighter of World War II. This plane's most recognizable feature was its inverted gull wing. In fact it was the Corsair's 2,000-hp Pratt & Whitney R-2800 engine, with its unique problems, that dictated the use of this type of wing. To take full advantage of such an immensely powerful engine, a huge, 13-foot-long propeller had to be used. This, however, would normally have required an unwieldy landing-gear strut over six feet long to provide ground clearance, which certainly would have created complications. Instead, Vought's design team ingeniously canted the center section of the wing downward, creating the inverted-gull-wing configuration. Now the landing-gear strut could be of a reasonable length, as the gull wing provided a low point for its attachment, while keeping the propeller high enough to clear the ground. Seen here are completed main spars of the wing center sections, the crux of the gull-wing arrangement. This was the most intricate, as well as the strongest, structure of the entire aircraft. *(Photo: National Air and Space Museum.)*

75. The Vought F4U forward-fuselage-and-inverted-gull-wing center section is seen in this 1944 photo in an early stage of assembly. Added benefits of the gull wing were that the tilted center section joined the two gull wings to the fuselage at the optimum angle for minimum drag and provided a low hinge line so the wings could be folded overhead. *(Photo: Cradle of Aviation Museum.)*

76. The Piper L-4, called the "Grasshopper," was the military version of the famous J-3 Cub Trainer. Built in Piper's Lock Haven, Pennsylvania, plant, the L-4 was constructed of a welded-steel-tubing fuselage, aluminum wing ribs and wooden spars. All was covered with cotton fabric sewed on, doped and painted. These women are "rib stitching," that is sewing the cotton covering to the aircraft's wing ribs. The L-4 was widely used for reconnaissance and artillery spotting in all theaters of the war. *(Photo: Cradle of Aviation Museum.)*

75

76

77

77. B-24 wing construction on an assembly line in San Diego. These workers are now riveting the skin on the outer wing panels. That was their sole function. In order to speed up production, complex jobs were broken down into 15 or 20 different operations. This easily permitted training a new worker to become an expert in one simplified job. The last B-24 off the San Diego assembly line was the 6,724th, completed on May 31, 1945. *(Photo: National Air and Space Museum.)*

Subcontractors and
Subassemblies

78.   The Republic P-47 Thunderbolt cowling, being
assembled here, was a NACA-design-type cowling
formed by four quick-detachable panels fastened to
support rings attached to the engine-valve-rocker
covers. Hydraulically operated cowling-ventilation
flaps were fitted at the rear. The front of the cowling
was formed (stamped) in a hydropress. The rest was
riveted on. *(Photo: Cradle of Aviation Museum.)*

78

79

80

79. This P-47 main fuel tank is being installed in the assembled fuselage. The 205-gallon self-sealing tank was situated forward of and below the cockpit between wing-hinge bulkheads. A 100-gallon auxiliary tank was directly aft of the rear wing-hinge support bulkhead. These self-sealing fuel tanks, developed by Goodyear, were a major innovation. Their special construction prevented bullets from igniting the fuel inside. They were made of chemigum, a combination of synthetic and soft natural rubber, reinforced with a specially developed high-tensile rayon-and-natural-fabric lining inside the tank. When a bullet punctured a tank lined with this material, contact with gasoline

caused the rubber to swell and seal the hole. Goodyear tanks were adopted as the standard cell for all types of combat aircraft. *(Photo: Cradle of Aviation Museum.)*

80. Halfway through the P-47D series, the bubble-canopy version was introduced in place of the "razor-back" version. The Plexiglas bubble canopy, seen here under construction at Republic, afforded all-around visibility, unlike the earlier razorback canopy, which had a blind spot to the rear. The Plexiglas canopy was molded in one piece and attached to a sliding aluminum frame. *(Photo: Cradle of Aviation Museum.)*

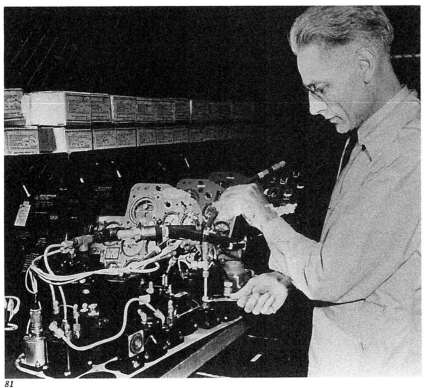

81

81. A precision worker delicately assembles an instrument panel for a P-47 Thunderbolt. Because of its complicated supercharger controls, the P-47 had more instruments than most other fighters. At the top center of the panel is the cutout for the gunsight, and the large instrument at its right is a Sperry Gyro-Horizon. *(Photo: Cradle of Aviation Museum.)*

82. Here, Plexiglas noses are being inspected for the A-20 midwing light bomber at the Douglas plant in El Segundo, California. Note one of the openings for the fixed forward machine guns. Developed from the earlier Douglas DB-7 design of 1937, and in production for foreign air forces in 1938, the A-20 was the most heavily produced Air Corps attack aircraft of World War II. Both France and England were operating DB-7's in numbers in 1939 and 1940. Initial Army contracts were for the A-20 version of the DB-7, which incorporated Wright R-2600 engines and increased armament. *(Photo: McDonnell Douglas Corp.)*

82

83

84

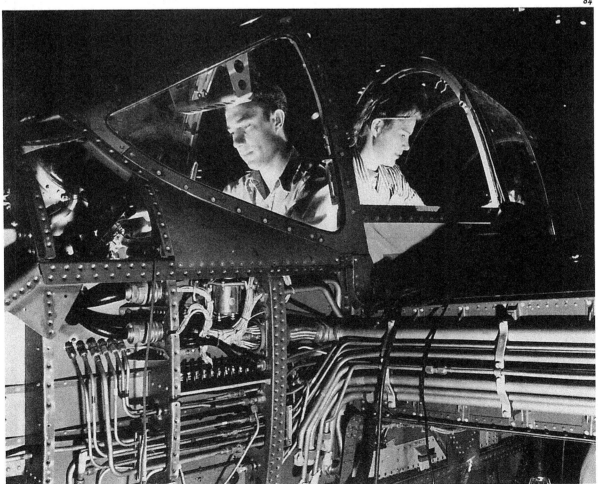

85

83. The enormous B-17 bomber contained literally miles of electrical wires, seen here being bundled. A complex variety of systems kept the B-17 flying. The flight controls were manually operated and included the ailerons, rudder, elevators, flaps and tabs. Most systems were electrically actuated: the hydraulic system controlled the cowl flaps on the engines, the emergency brakes and the wheel brakes. The communications system on the B-17 was also extremely complicated, for not only were the crew members in communication with each other, but the pilot and radio operator were also in touch with the formation and the base. The electrical system also furnished the power to operate the turrets, landing gear, wing flaps, bomb doors, instruments and other equipment. *(Photo: National Air and Space Museum.)*

84. Interior fittings being installed in a P-38 cockpit assembly. The part normally called the fuselage, which in the P-38 was merely the cockpit and armament nacelle, was built in two halves attached along a vertical joint, facilitating structural assembly as well as the installation of functional parts such as controls, plumbing and electrical equipment. The cockpit enclosure had side panels, which could be lowered by the pilot, and a top-center transparent panel hinged at the aft end to permit egress. The pilot was protected by a bulletproof glass windscreen, armor plate on the aft end of the armament compartment, armor on his seat bottom and back and another piece of armor plate behind the seat. *(Photo: National Art and Space Museum.)*

85. An initial order for 286 Grumman TBF "Avenger" torpedo bombers was placed three days after the second prototype's maiden flight, and the first production aircraft was handed over to the U.S. Navy at the end of January 1942. Production built up quickly, a total of 145 Avengers being delivered by the end of June 1942. Grumman had built 2,293 TBF's when in December 1943 it turned Avenger production over to the Eastern Aircraft Division of General Motors so Grumman could concentrate on Hellcat production and experimental work. GM ultimately produced 7,546 Avengers as the TBM. The Avenger on the left is having its engine-to-aircraft connections made and its bomb-bay doors installed. The Avenger on the right has just received its horizontal stabilizer and is now having some work done in the tail-hook area. *(Photo: Grumman Corporation.)*

86. Manufacturing C-47 landing-gear struts at the Dowty Equipment Company, Long Island City, New York. The Dowty Company, established in 1939, was a subsidiary of the Dowty Company of England. They produced only hydraulic pumps and landing-gear struts. Dowty was just one of several thousand little-known highly specialized subcontractors who supplied the major manufacturers with the wide assortment of parts they needed. Here, the struts are being sprayed with a corrosion-resistant primer, most likely zinc chromate. *(Photo: Cradle of Aviation Museum.)*

87. Fuel and air for the engine were combined and regulated by the carburetor. One of the most common types of aircraft carburetors during the war was the Stromberg injection carburetor, seen here during assembly in Stromberg's Chicago plant. In the injection carburetor, fuel was atomized and forced through orifices by "air venturi suction." This system had several advantages in that it prevented carburetor icing and negated the effects of gravity and inertia. These PD-12 throttle body units show the two large openings on top for the venturi tubes and a large opening in front for the fuel-control unit. Inside was a large butterfly-type throttle valve. *(Photo: Cradle of Aviation Museum.)*

87

86

88

89

88. The Hamilton Standard counterweight propeller was one of three controllable-pitch propellers used by American aircraft in World War II (Hydromatic and Curtiss-Electric were the others). The Hamilton Standard propeller had a counterweight assembly attached to each blade, which was used to change the angle of the blades. Here, blades made by Chevrolet (for Hamilton Standard) in Saginaw, Michigan, are being "aged" in an oven for 16 hours. The heat-treating process gave the steel blades great strength. Contrary to usual practice, the 175-foot-long furnace was hung from the ceiling to save floor space. *(Photo: Cradle of Aviation Museum.)*

89. These blades are being "normalized" after welding. They were held very compactly while being hauled in and out of the cylindrical electric furnace. The man on the left is controlling the hoist electrically. *(Photo: Cradle of Aviation Museum.)*

90.

90. The center of each Hamilton Standard counter-weight propeller had a hydraulic cylinder mounted ahead of the hub. The blades were normally in high pitch because the counterweights were forced outward by centrifugal force. Adding oil to the hydraulic cylinder through the crankshaft forced the blades into low pitch. Here, prior to completion, a three-blade propeller receives its final polishing at the Hamilton Standard plant near Hartford, Connecticut. *(Photo: Cradle of Aviation Museum.)*

91. The Pratt & Whitney R-1830 engine, named the "Twin Wasp," was a 14-cylinder, two-row radial engine. A classic engine, the 1,200-hp R-1830 was one of the best all-around radial engines ever built. Here, at the

Pratt & Whitney plant in East Hartford, Connecticut, thousands of Twin Wasp cylinders are readied for the assembly line. The cast-aluminum fins, a miracle of foundry technique, were as little as $\frac{1}{16}$-inch thick. *(Photo: Cradle of Aviation Museum.)*

92. The Pratt & Whitney R-1830 was used in the Grumman F4F Wildcat and Consolidated B-24 Liberator, among others. It had what was probably the world's first two-stage supercharger. Engine assembly hit a peak of 3,377 at the East Hartford plant in March 1943. Here, completed Twin Wasps are lifted from assembly stands to shipping crates. *(Photo: Cradle of Aviation Museum.)*

93.   An extremely important engine during the war was the Pratt & Whitney R-2800 "Double Wasp," America's first 18-cylinder radial. Heat dissipation in this 2,000-hp engine proved to be a problem; thus, cast or forged cooling fins could not be used. The cooling fins needed were so thin and fine-pitched that instead they had to be machined from the solid metal of the head forging. They were cut all at once on a row of automated milling saws. The cylinders were made of two sections. Here, the body can be seen being carefully screwed onto the cylinder head at Pratt & Whitney's East Hartford Plant. *(Photo: Cradle of Aviation Museum.)*

94.   The R-2800 obtained 2,000 hp from 2,800 cubic inches—no other air-cooled engine came close to this figure. It was uprated to 2,400 hp late in the war. However, this big engine never went into a heavy bomber. It was a power plant exclusively for fighters and medium bombers. It was used in the P-47, F6F, F4U, B-26 and A-26. Here, at Ford's Dearborn, Michigan, plant in 1944, R-2800's built under license are nearing completion on the "Green" assembly line. The engines are mounted on moving cradles that can be tipped at all angles for adding parts. *(Photo: Cradle of Aviation Museum.)*

95.   One of the largest landing-gear assemblies produced during the war was the massive B-29 main gear. Made by Smith in Milwaukee, it consisted of a single oleo (hydraulic) strut with dual wheels. Each main gear weighed 2,615 pounds and would absorb an impact load of 200,000 pounds. Attached to the rear wing spar, the strut was compressed by the airplane's weight when it touched the ground. The wheels consisted of magnesium hubs with 56-inch-diameter 18-ply nylon tires. This completed assembly, dwarfing a worker, is being "rolled out" on a handling dolly. *(Photo: Cradle of Aviation Museum.)*

96.   One of the few things common to World War II aircraft was that they generally all needed the same types of instruments. The major instrument makers during the war were Sperry, Kollsman and Pioneer, all located on Long Island, New York. Eventually all of their designs were subcontracted to other makers in order to keep up with the demand. With rapidly increasing orders, Sperry went from 5,582 employees in 1940 to 32,397 in 1943. Here, mostly women workers calibrate Gyro-Compasses at Sperry's Lake Success, New York, plant. The Gyro-Compass gave a more accurate directional reading than the magnetic compass. *(Photo: Cradle of Aviation Museum.)*

93

95

94

96

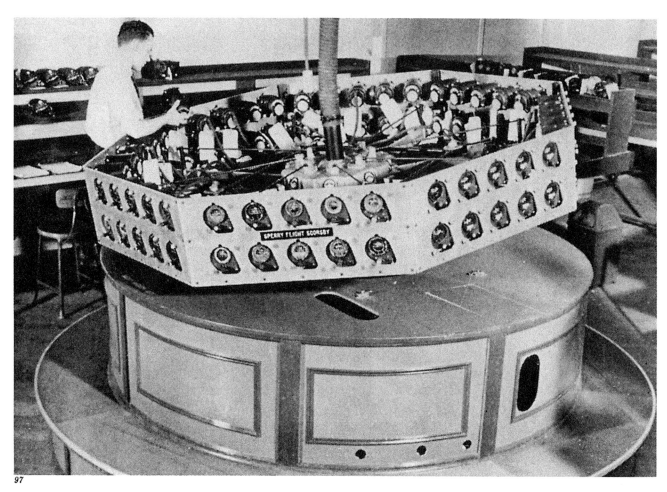

97

98

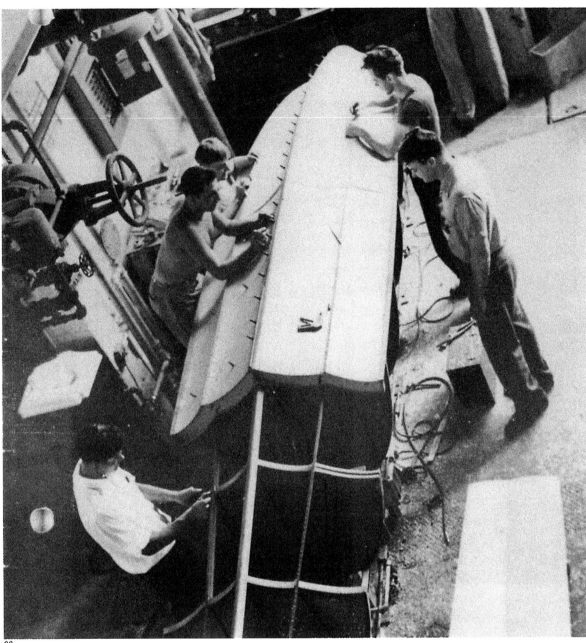

99

97. Eighty Sperry Gyro-Horizons "take off" during a shop test checking them for accuracy of indication. The Gyro-Horizon showed the aircraft's attitude in flight. Between late 1941 and late 1943 Sperry built 124,000 Gyro-Horizons and 110,000 Gyro-Compasses. The Gyro-Compasses were eventually subcontracted to Chrysler. Sperry also built the S-1 bombsight on Long Island. *(Photo: Cradle of Aviation Museum.)*

98. In order to ensure that the instruments would work at great altitude, some were periodically taken off the assembly line and tested in Sperry's high-altitude pressure chamber. Inspectors wore warm clothes and oxygen masks to protect them from the low temperatures and lack of oxygen at simulated high altitudes. In all, Sperry built over 400,000 flight instruments during World War II. *(Photo: Cradle of Aviation Museum.)*

99. Aircraft-float production at the EDO plant, College Point, Long Island, New York. The EDO Corpora-tion, founded in 1925, was, and still is, the largest producer of aircraft floats in the world. EDO produced virtually every float used by the Navy and Air Corps in World War II. Most of their production was of the Model 68 float for the Vought OS2U "Kingfisher," seen here under construction. EDO built a total of 1,200 Kingfisher floats with a work force that peaked at 2,440. They also built the Model 78 float for the C-47, the largest aircraft float ever built. Of the several observation and scouting aircraft available to the Navy when the U.S. entered World War II, the Vought Kingfisher was to prove the most useful. Kingfishers saw extensive use as observation and air/sea rescue aircraft, so the EDO floats had to be able to take a pounding in the heavy surf off Pacific islands. Barely visible in the bottom half of the photo are the solid, watertight vertical bulkheads attached by the center keel and two sister keelsons. Upon completion, each section of the float was filled with water and checked for any signs of leakage. *(Photo: EDO Corporation.)*

Tail Assemblies

100

100. The tail surfaces of the Republic P-47 were assembled as one unit and then bolted onto the fuselage as seen here. The fin and horizontal stabilizer were structures of stamped ribs, secured fore and aft to spars and covered with alclad skin, flush-riveted. The rudder and elevators were covered with aluminum, not fabric, as the P-47 could approach the speed of sound in a dive and compression would have torn the fabric off. Engine exhaust gases were released through the butterfly valve housed in the stainless-steel hood, visible here under the rear fuselage. *(Photo: Cradle of Aviation Museum.)*

101. Mounting the elevators on a Boeing B-17F. The tail section of the Flying Fortress consisted of two horizontal stabilizers and two elevators, as well as the vertical fin on top of the fuselage and the rudder hinged to the fin. The horizontal and vertical stabilizers directed the movement of air caused by the forward motion of the plane and the slip stream from the

propeller so that it flowed evenly over the movable control surfaces that maneuvered the plane. The stabilizers consisted of aluminum spars and a series of stamped aluminum ribs placed at intervals to form the shape of and give the proper strength to the stabilizers. All control surfaces were fabric-covered. Note the massiveness of the fin and rudder. The rear section with the tail guns will be attached next. *(Photo: Cradle of Aviation Museum.)*

102. The two booms of the Lockheed P-38 supported the entire tail assembly. The two-piece fins were mounted on the tailcones, which also supported both ends of the horizontal stabilizer. The aluminum-covered and flush-riveted rudders were divided into upper and lower halves. The entire tail assembly was constructed as a unit and mounted onto the tail booms. Thus it was also easily detachable for repair. *(Photo: Cradle of Aviation Museum.)*

104

103. The B-24 "Liberator" tail assembly at the Consolidated Vultee plant in Fort Worth. The B-24 had twin tails attached to a horizontal stabilizer, all of which attached to the aircraft in a single unit. Elevators were attached to the trailing edge of the stabilizer. Each fin had an aerodynamically balanced rudder attached at the rear. Elevators and rudders on the B-24 were of aluminum-rib-and-spar construction, fabric-covered. All the main sections of the B-24 were fabricated in advance as subassemblies before they reached the final assembly line. From the subassembly area in this photo, the tails will move to the final-assembly area, where they will be attached to the fuselage by four large bolts. Each B-24 contained 102,000 separate parts, not counting 85,000 nuts and bolts and 400,000 rivets. *(Photo: National Air and Space Museum.)*

104. B-29 "Superfortress" fins at the Briggs plant in Detroit, awaiting shipment. To feed Boeing's prime airframe assembly of the B-29 in four plants, the largest aircraft subcontracting program ever undertaken was set up throughout the country for B-29 equipment and subassemblies. *(Photo: Cradle of Aviation Museum.)*

Mating Wings

105. Early model P-47D's undergoing final assembly at Republic in April 1944. The wings will next be "mated" to the fuselage in the foreground. Landing gear will be added next, and the engine cowling and propeller will be attached last. Note in the rear some wings with British markings (hard to see in the photograph) and fuselages stored vertically to save space. *(Photo: Cradle of Aviation Museum.)*

106. Attaching the wing to a P-47D "Thunderbolt." The suspended wing will be bolted to the fuselage at four attach points using tapered bolts. The turbosupercharger ducts are just visible on the underside. The landing gear has not yet been attached. *(Photo: Cradle of Aviation Museum.)*

107. Developed from a commercial design, the Lockheed 14 transport—the "Hudson"—was originally converted to a military aircraft in order to meet British requirements for a coastal reconnaissance bomber. It was also used by the U.S. Army Air Corps as the A-29, and this type made the first successful attack on a U-boat by an American Army plane in World War II. This Hudson fuselage is about to be lowered onto its wing center section from an overhead conveyor at the Lockheed Burbank plant. The workers beneath are checking for the exact alignment necessary. The flight deck can just be seen through the open nose section. *(Photo: National Air and Space Museum.)*

106

107

108

109

108. Completed PBY outer wing sections are suspended on overhead conveyors at the Consolidated factory in San Diego. The PBY "Catalina" had a parasol-mounted wing with largely internal bracing, thus nearly making it a true cantilever wing. Adding to its aerodynamic cleanness was the incorporation of unique retractable stabilizing floats that folded upward to become the wingtips in flight in order to reduce drag. The PBY's wings (actually one continuous wing) consisted of two outer panels and a center section with a streamlined structure attached to the hull. The aft portion of the wing, as well as the ailerons, was fabric-covered. All aluminum parts on the PBY were protected from salt corrosion by an anodic treatment immediately prior to the application of the priming coat. This 1938 photo of Consolidated's plant reveals that the PBY was already in mass production. With the outbreak of war in Europe, the demand for PBY's increased rapidly. Canada, Australia and Britain all ordered Catalinas in quantity. On December 20, 1939, the U.S. Navy ordered 200 PBY's, primarily to equip the Neutrality Patrol. *(Photo: National Air and Space Museum.)*

109. The Brewster F2A "Buffalo" featured a short stubby fuselage and the shortest wing of any American fighter of the Second World War. The mid-mounted one-piece wing had one gun on each side. There were also two guns in the cowling. Setting up Brewster's Rube Goldberg production line created many problems, severely hindering their delivery schedule. The first F2A was finished in July 1939 but Brewster was unable to complete enough planes to outfit a squadron until the following December. Here a Buffalo receives its wing with its hydraulically operated split flaps lowered. This plane was part of an export order for the Dutch. *(Photo: Jim Maas.)*

110. Mating the inboard wing of a Boeing B-17 to the fuselage. The built-up truss-type front spar is plainly evident. The corrugated inner reinforcement of the wing's skin is just visible in the upper left. Note all of the large spaces left open for the exacting mating process. *(Photo: National Air and Space Museum.)*

111. The Curtiss C-46 "Commando" one-piece wing was built in three sections, an untapered center section and two outer panels with detachable tips. The center section, being attached here, ran through the fuselage just below the cabin floor. Three spars were utilized in this section, with engine nacelles and landing-gear fittings attached to the front spar. Built as separate assemblies, which could be changed in service if necessary, the engine nacelles were riveted to the center section. *(Photo: National Air and Space Museum.)*

110

111

112. In final assembly in Buffalo, these C-46's are now receiving their outer wing panels. The removable outer panels were attached to the center section just outboard of the engine nacelles by special high-strength bolts encircling the wing through a splice plate. Wing ribs were web-truss type, formed in one hydropress operation, the cutouts being blanked and a bead for added stiffness being put in during one press stroke. Only the ailerons were fabric-covered. Note the P-40's in final assembly in the foreground. A simple row of metal shelving divides the two lines in the crowded plant. *(Photo: National Air and Space Museum.)*

113

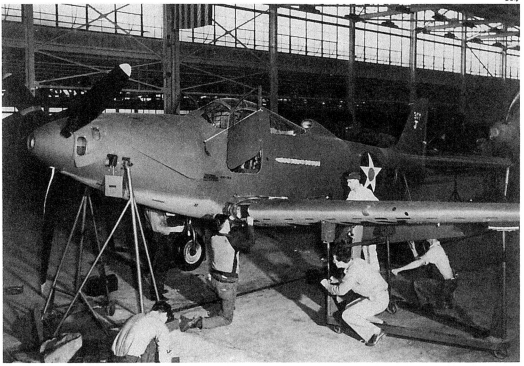

114

113. P-38 "Lightning" assembly line at Lockheed's Burbank, California, plant. This stage of assembly, which was peculiar to the P-38, was known as the body-assembly or body-mating operation. At this point the mated center sections (in the rear) and the completed fuselages were attached, and the assembly known as the forward booms was attached to the center section along with the engines. The outer wing panels were also mated to the center section. The outer wings included the leading edge, wingtip, aileron and flap. Each leading-edge assembly held a self-sealing fuel tank. The wing panels each consisted of two spars, pressed ribs and stressed-skin covering. Forty-five Lightnings are visible in just this one photo, plus "Hudsons" in the rear and on the left side. *(Photo: Cradle of Aviation Museum.)*

114. Mounting P-39 "Airacobra" wings at the Bell Buffalo plant. The P-39's wing center section was built as an integral part of the forward fuselage. The outer wing panels are being joined to the center section with 30 bolts in each splice. The wing panels were each formed of three spars and 13 ribs. The skin was reinforced with drawn aluminum stringers and was entirely flush-riveted. Note the tricycle landing gear lowered and the open automobile-type cockpit door. *(Photo: National Air and Space Museum.)*

Engine Installation

115

115. Initial preparation prior to mounting an 18-cylinder 2,000-hp Pratt & Whitney R-2800 engine in a Republic P-47 "Thunderbolt." The R-2800 was the most powerful, and probably the most reliable, engine mounted in an American fighter during World War II. In order to take full advantage of the power of the R-2800, the P-47 became the first U.S. fighter to mount a massive 12-foot, four-bladed controllable-pitch propeller. Using such a large propeller meant the first use of telescoping landing gear. The gear would lengthen nine inches when lowered in order to provide enough ground clearance. When raised, it shortened in order to fit in the wing and leave enough room for the guns. *(Photo: Cradle of Aviation Museum.)*

116

116.   The P-47's fully assembled R-2800 engine on its mount with all accessories. Note the large 28-gallon oil tank on top and the two turbosupercharger ducts on the bottom. The P-47 had a General Electric exhaust-driven turbosupercharger located in the lower fuselage, 21 feet aft of the propeller. The exhaust gases were ducted to the turbo through insulated pipes, one on each side of the lower fuselage. Air for supercharging reached the turbo through a long duct from the lower engine cowl. After supercharging, the air passed through an intercooler prior to being piped back along either side of the fuselage to a single carburetor intake. *(Photo: Cradle of Aviation Museum.)*

117.   The Curtiss C-46 was powered by two 2,000-hp Pratt & Whitney R-2800 engines. The engines were attached to a firewall of light-gauge stainless steel backed by asbestos sheet and aluminum-alloy sheet. As seen in this photo, to facilitate maintenance, this portion of the C-46 was designed so that the entire power plant—engine mount, firewall and all accessories forward of the firewall—could be removed, or as here, mounted, in one unit. *(Photo: National Air and Space Museum.)*

118.   Now on the main assembly line, these Curtiss P-40E fuselages are receiving their engine mounts, engines and all accessories. The fuselage was of conventional bulkhead-and-stringer construction, covered by aluminum-alloy sheet. It was also built in two halves to speed production time, the lower being trundled under the upper and the completed shell moved on along the production line. The P-40 series was powered by an Allison V-1710 12-cylinder engine of 960 hp. The engine mount consisted of a forked welded-steel tubing structure flattened at the ends and bolted together with the engine mounting-flange plates. *(Photo: National Air and Space Museum.)*

117

118

B8-18554-SN
1-25-43

119

119. Because of the enormous demands on production facilities as a result of foreign and American orders, in 1941 Curtiss expanded its production capability by 400 percent. Total employment now stood at 45,000. A second factory built in Buffalo was known as Plant Two and meant an additional 1.2 million square feet of space. Curtiss also expanded its St. Louis plant to 1.2 million square feet. Output at the St. Louis plant was over six aircraft per day while the entire Curtiss airplane division ultimately produced sixty airplanes per day. The crowded conditions in the final assembly area of Plant Two give some idea of the capacity here. Bare P-40 fuselages are seen on the right. Toward the left they may be seen receiving their windscreen, canopy, engine and cowling. Curtiss O-52 "Owl" observation planes are being assembled in the foreground. Curtiss built 203 O-52's for the Air Corps, but the type was deemed unfit for combat and was relegated to duties within the U.S. *(Photo: Cradle of Aviation Museum.)*

120. Lockheed's P-38 was powered by two Allison V-1710 12-cylinder liquid-cooled engines of 1,500 hp each, seen here being mounted. They turned three-blade Curtiss electric propellers. Twin tail booms were selected for the P-38 as the logical extension of the engine nacelles, simply made longer to house the superchargers and carry the tail. *(Photo: National Air and Space Museum.)*

121. Hanging the engine in a P-38 nearing final assembly. The breakdown of assembly in the Lightning allowed the installation of the functional parts of the airplane in the early stages of assembly. For example, the entire cooling system was installed in the aft booms at the time they were assembled in their respective jigs and work stations. *(Photo: National Air and Space Museum.)*

120

121

122

123

124

122. The Martin B-26 "Marauder" contract was won in 1939 in an industry-wide competition for a new medium-size bomber. The B-26 had the Air Corps' first power-operated turret, the first all-plastic bombardier's nose and one of the first tail turrets. It also had the highest wing loading of any aircraft designed for the Air Corps to this time and, in consequence, had very high takeoff and landing speeds. The B-26 was built primarily in Baltimore, Maryland, but Martin set up a second B-26 assembly line near Omaha, Nebraska. After 1,500 were built here production was shifted to B-29's (the *Enola Gay* was an Omaha-built Martin B-29). The majority of the B-26's built saw service either in Europe, the Mediterranean or the Southwest Pacific. A total of 5,266 B-26's were built at a cost of $217,000 each. The twin-engine bomber was powered by two 2,000-hp Pratt & Whitney R-2800 engines, seen here being readied for mounting on a B-26. *(Photo: National Air and Space Museum.)*

123. Eighteen-cylinder 2,000-hp Pratt & Whitney R-2800's being readied for installation in F4U "Cor-
sairs" at Vought's Stratford, Connecticut, plant. The exhaust system of this engine was unique in that it utilized the energy of the exhaust gases, including their jet effect, for propulsion. Six separate exhaust manifolds (seen on the engine at the left), each serving three cylinders, discharged the exhaust backwards under the fuselage and created at full throttle a force equal to an additional 210 hp and an extra 20 mph. The Corsair thus showed the first application of the jet-thrust principle in a radial, air-cooled high-performance aircraft. *(Photo: National Air and Space Museum.)*

124. At the outbreak of the war the Grumman F4F "Wildcat" was the only Navy fighter on hand that was capable of offering any resistance to the Japanese attackers. Different versions of the F4F mounted either four or six .50-caliber machine guns in the wings. This F4F-3 is just now receiving its Pratt & Whitney engine. Note how the engine, cowling and engine mount are being attached as one unit. *(Photo: Grumman Corporation.)*

125. The series of Vultee low-wing trainers produced by Vultee Aircraft of Nashville, Tennessee, from 1940 to 1944, by far outnumbered all other aircraft in the basic-training category. It served almost exclusively as the basic type for all air crews trained in the U.S. during World War II. Vultee's BT-13 "Valiant" was a docile monoplane of all-metal construction, except for fabric-covered movable tail surfaces. The BT-13 basic trainer represented the second of the three training stages—primary, basic and advanced—common to all training programs. The BT-13 was normally equipped with a 450-hp Pratt & Whitney R-985 engine, seen here. Various engine accessories are being installed by these

women at Vultee's Nashville plant, and a firewall can be seen behind each. Note how the engines are attached to an overhead tramrail. *(Photo: National Air and Space Museum.)*

126. So rapid was the buildup of BT-13 production that engine production could not keep pace. Thus 1,700 were ordered as BT-15's with Wright R-975 engines. These BT-13's are receiving their engines from a drop-section tramrail. The overhead carrier delivered the engines and automatically returned to the engine-assembly area (the area seen in the previous photo). *(Photo: Cradle of Aviation Museum.)*

Armament

127

127. During World War II the Martin Company of Baltimore became the world's largest manufacturer of power-operated turrets for aircraft. Their model 250 CE was the most widely used, over 40,000 having been manufactured and used on 12 different aircraft. The Martin PBM "Mariner" was the first American flying boat equipped with a turret. Each turret mounted two .50-caliber machine guns. The turrets in this photo will be installed on the Mariner fuselages seen in the rear. *(Photo: National Air and Space Museum.)*

128. The armament of the P-39 was unique. It consisted of a 37mm cannon located on the fuselage centerline just above the extension drive shaft, with the gun barrel projecting through the reduction gearbox and propeller hub. Two .50-caliber machine guns were also installed in the forward fuselage ahead of the pilot, firing through the propeller, and four .30-caliber machine guns were installed in pairs in the outer wing panels. The 37mm cannon was fed from a circular endless-belt-type magazine installed around the cannon and containing 30 rounds. Here a Bell worker installs the cannon barrel directly through the propeller hub. *(Photo: National Air and Space Museum.)*

128

129. Attaching the rocket pylons to a nearly complete Grumman F6F-5 "Hellcat." The Hellcat could carry six 6-inch-diameter unguided solid-fuel rockets primarily to be used against shipping and land-based targets. In addition to rockets, it had six .50-caliber machine guns with 400 rounds of ammunition for each gun. Armor plate protected the oil tank, fuel tank and pilot. The Hellcat was used primarily in the Pacific by Navy and Marine units. In this photo, the machine-gun tubes have been masked so the aircraft can be painted in the next station. *(Photo: Grumman Corporation.)*

129

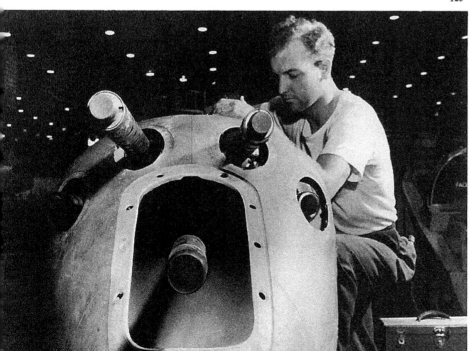

130. Armament being installed in the business end of the Lockheed P-38. The armament of the P-38 was unusual in that four .50-caliber machine guns and one 20mm cannon were placed in the nose, firing from within a 20-inch-diameter space. This proved very effective, as the effect of having a small number of guns was counteracted by their concentration in the fuselage where they could fire straight ahead rather than having their firepower converge from the wings. Placing all the guns in the nose was also very effective inasmuch as the firepower was all ahead of the pilot and just below his line of vision. *(Photo: National Air and Space Museum.)*

130

131. The Northrop P-61 "Black Widow" night fighter had a power turret on top of the fuselage carrying four .50-caliber machine guns, which was operated by a gunner located in the aft part of the fuselage. Normally the turret was locked in the forward-firing position to supplement the plane's four cannons. The early P-61A's were delivered with this turret, but a tail-buffeting problem was traced to the turret and later P-61A's were delivered without it. The first 200 P-61B's were also delivered without the turret, but the buffeting was soon corrected and the turrets were installed on the 201st P-61B and all production thereafter. These workers at Northrop's Hawthorne, California, plant are adjusting the top turret after installation. *(Photo: Cradle of Aviation Museum.)*

132. The most commonly used aircraft machine gun during the war was the .50-caliber Browning M2HB. Built by Colt and Marlin in Connecticut, the gun evolved from the M2 water-cooled, and later air-cooled, ground machine gun. Cooling problems due to the powerful .50 cartridge led to the development of the M2HB (heavy barrel) during the 1930's, which was capable of absorbing more heat and dissipating it faster. This permitted longer firing periods without the danger of overheating. This version was for fixed and flexible aircraft use. Here workers complete the heavy 65-pound guns by attaching the ammunition chutes. The air-cooling holes in the barrel are plainly visible. *(Photo: Cradle of Aviation Museum.)*

131

132

133. Once completed, Republic P-47's were test-fitted with their .50-caliber machine guns. This worker is fitting the main body of the gun into specially designed Republic gun mounts. The gun bays in the wings were situated outboard of the undercarriage well and actuating gear. Note the staggered arrangement for the machine guns, which allowed ammunition-feed troughs to be arranged side by side in the outer wing panels. *(Photo: Cradle of Aviation Museum.)*

134. The machine guns in completed P-47's were always test-fired to ensure proper alignment and accuracy. The Republic P-47 "Thunderbolt" had four .50-caliber machine guns in each wing, the most firepower of any American fighter in the Second World War. Ammunition boxes containing 350 rounds per gun were located outboard of the guns. *(Photo: Cradle of Aviation Museum.)*

133

134

135.

135. In the late 1930's and early 1940's, when the B-17 and B-24 were under development, Sperry on Long Island was contracted by the Air Corps to design and build a new type of gunner's turret for these aircraft. Thus Sperry developed an armor-plated "ball turret" to protect the underside of these large bombers from attacks by enemy fighters. The Type A-2 Lower Gun Turret was an armor-plated sphere 44 inches in diameter that mounted two .50-caliber machine guns. The turret was supported by a framework suspended from inside the top of the fuselage. The guns were fixed in relation to the turret, but an electro-hydraulic unit enabled the turret to rotate in any direction. In the event of power failure it could be moved manually. After initial development and production, Sperry subcontracted ball-turret production to Briggs, whose factory is seen here. The turret continued to be known as the "Sperry ball," however. Note the large mounting ring positioned vertically on the assembly line. *(Photo: Cradle of Aviation Museum.)*

136

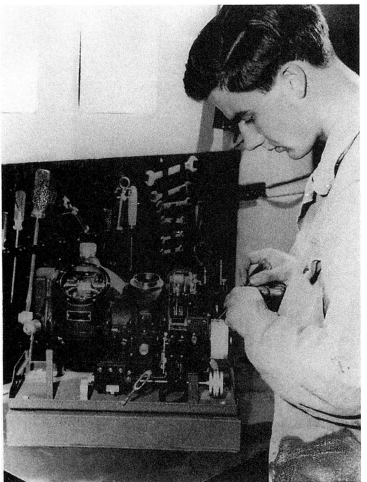

137

136. In the ball turret, the gunner was housed inside the spherical structure, surrounded by ½-inch-thick armor plate provided for his protection (giving the turret a total weight of 850 pounds). The gunner sighted through an automatic Sperry sight and the turret, guns, sight and gunner moved as a unit while tracking the target. Plexiglas windows gave the gunner a wide field of vision and he had a circular sighting window of bulletproof glass directly in front of him. The turret rotated on both the vertical and horizontal axis in order to aim the guns. It could rotate 90 degrees vertically and 360 degrees horizontally at 45 degrees per second. This Sperry ball has just been mated to the belly of a B-24. Note the open gunner's door and circular sighting window. *(Photo: Cradle of Aviation Museum.)*

137. Famous for its accuracy, the Norden bombsight was an "open secret" during World War II. Everyone had heard of it, yet until 1945, practically no one outside the military had ever seen a picture of it. In technical terms, it could place a bomb load inside a 100-foot-diameter circle from four miles up. Actually the sight was only the aiming device. To correct for draft, maintain altitude, adjust airspeed and control the aircraft, Norden developed a gyro-stabilized automatic pilot. The bombardier needed only to make several calculations and adjustments, and the automatic pilot would fly the plane and release the bombs. Thus the Norden sight was on an analog computer that solved the geometry of bomb ballistics with cranked-in data for airspeed, altitude, drift and heading. By the end of the war, more than 25,000 bombsights had been built by Norden in New York City, and thousands more by subcontractors. Each had cost the government $10,000. Here, a Norden sight receives its final adjustments before leaving the plant. *(Photo: Norden Systems, United Technologies.)*

Painting

138

139

92

140

138. Stenciling the Air Corps serial number onto a shiny new P-47 Thunderbolt. Not only was massive P-47 production going on at Republic's Farmingdale, Long Island, New York, plant, but their Evansville, Indiana, plant was also producing over 50 planes per month. By the spring of 1944 Evansville was accounting for 40 percent of all Thunderbolt production. Later model P-47's were left unpainted, in contrast to the earlier models, which were painted olive drab. *(Photo: Cradle of Aviation Museum.)*

139. A completed Grumman F6F Hellcat is given its white natural-star markings. The plane has already been painted in its three-color scheme and the areas shown here are being masked off to prevent overspray. Perhaps the most important claim for the Hellcat was that it outperformed the Japanese "Zero" in nearly every department. Of equal importance, the F6F needed few modifications and practically no structural changes during its production lifetime. It was such a fine design that, structurally, the 12,000th Hellcat was the same as the first, something highly unusual in the aircraft industry. *(Photo: Grumman Corporation.)*

140. Among the innovative developments that speeded construction of Piper L-4's was the "Ferris wheel" in the finishing room. Similar in many ways to the regular fairground wheel, the device had the capacity of twelve wings and six fuselages. As the wheel rotated, workmen sprayed the units with dope and paint. By the time a unit completed one cycle, it had dried and was ready for a second painting. Piper was also among the first to introduce an overhead conveyor system to step up production. Serving as air observation posts, L-4's had at their command the most formidable array of guns in the history of warfare. *(Photo: Cradle of Aviation Museum.)*

Final Assembly

141. By 1940 the Curtiss P-40 "Warhawk" was unquestionably inferior at high altitude to the more modern turbosupercharged designs, but it was cheaper and, being based on an airframe design proven in mass production, could be produced in quantity a full year ahead of any other type. With the urgent need for a modern fighter in the shortest possible time, the Army acted to obtain the P-40 for the imminent crisis. Thus in April 1939 Curtiss was awarded a contract for 524 P-40's at a cost of $12,872,898. This was the largest single contract for aircraft since the end of World War I. These P-40B's nearing final assembly in Buffalo in 1941 represent the earlier models in the P-40 series. The P-40B featured several improvements over the previous model, the P-40A. The landing-gear fairing and oil cooler were completely redesigned, and this version now carried two .50-caliber guns in the nose and two .30-caliber guns in each wing. These aircraft are also being fitted with constant-speed three-bladed all-metal electrically controlled Curtiss propellers. *(Photo: National Air and Space Museum.)*

141

142

142. Five separate final-assembly lines are visible in this photo of the Curtiss factory in Buffalo. The P-40 fuselages are now being mated to their wings. The P-40 wings were joined as one piece, each made of four sections consisting of two main panels and two wingtips. Wing construction was multispar, with ribs made of stamped aluminum sheet. The P-40 fuselage was lowered onto the wing and bolted into place at the centerline of the fuselage through heavy bolt angles attached to the wing. The wing-to-fuselage join was then covered with large sheet fairing strips riveted to contour ribs that extended from the fuselage bulkheads. Note the export British P-40's being assembled in the rear. *(Photo: Cradle of Aviation Museum.)*

143

144

145

143. In 1939 the U.S. Navy issued a specification for a new monoplane dive-bomber replacement for the SBC "Helldiver" biplane. Curtiss quickly responded and the SB2C Helldiver was ordered in May 1939. Since the Buffalo plants were already overcrowded, Curtiss established a new 1.1 million-square-foot factory in Columbus, Ohio, just for Helldiver production. Production here was protracted, however, and the first deliveries did not take place until December 1942. Part of the problem with the SB2C was that the original Navy requirement called for a dive bomber with a large internal bomb bay but small enough for two planes to fit onto a standard aircraft-carrier elevator. The usual solution to the need for a large internal capacity is to make a bigger aircraft, but Curtiss was restricted in this area. Thus they developed an aircraft that was extremely broad for its length and with an increased tail area. This gave the aircraft an awkward appearance as well as a general instability. Here, uprated SB2C-3's with the big Wright R-2600 "Double Cyclone" and four-bladed propellers are nearing completion on Curtiss' Columbus assembly line in 1943. (Photo: National Air and Space Museum.)

144. Although obsolete by the end of 1940, the Brewster F2A was kept in production, as the Navy needed fighters, good ones or not. Grumman F4F's could not be produced fast enough, so the "Buffalo" remained in production through 1941. One of the major defects the Buffalo suffered from was landing-gear failure. The "vee" structure of the gear struts was inherently weak, and the stress of arrested carrier landings was more than they could stand. This export British Buffalo is undergoing a landing-gear-retraction test at Brewster's final-assembly hangar at Long Island's Roosevelt Field. (Photo: Jim Maas.)

145. Final assembly of the very large Lockheed P-38 was crowded out of the bulging Burbank factory and kept outdoors in the mild California weather. (This view dates from 1944.) Aluminum alloy, alclad and stainless steel were the basic materials most commonly used in airframes. Alclad was used for skin covering. Aluminum alloy was used for ribs, structural parts of wings and fuselages, cowlings and longerons. Stainless steel was used for parts, such as engine mounts and firewalls, that had to withstand high temperatures. Even the basic components of the airframe were subdivided into many intricate parts. For example, in the wingtip of the P-38, to be mounted on the left, there were 14 pieces of tubing, ribs and sheet skin, and 277 nuts and bolts, plus hundreds of rivets. (Photo: National Air and Space Museum.)

KEEP CLEAR FOR PITOT TUBE

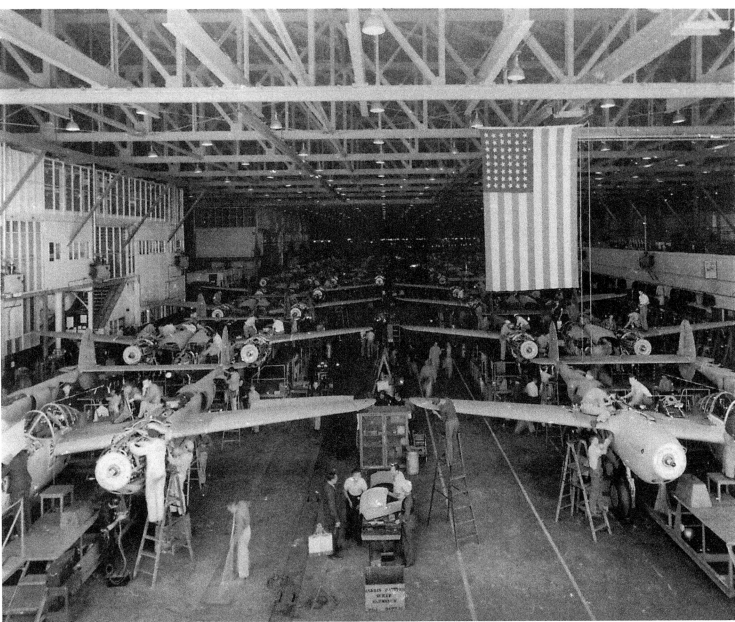

148

146. The forward booms and center sections of the P-38 together carried the landing gear and power plants. After removal from the body jig, the airplane was moved to its final-assembly station, seen here. The sequence of assembly from this point to final acceptance started with the installation of the aft booms and tail group, after which the outer wing panels, landing gear and power plants were installed. Note the row of soon-to-be-installed Allison engines on the right. *(Photo: National Air and Space Museum.)*

147. Final assembly of "Lightnings" at Lockheed's Burbank plant, in 1944. Note the airscoops for the superchargers and engine coolant on the outside of the aft tail booms. The superchargers were of the General Electric exhaust-driven turbo type, just visible above and behind the rear beam of the wing mounted in the forward booms. The parts-supply line, between the assembly lines, feeding components to the Lightnings as needed, is clearly visible. *(Photo: National Air and Space Museum.)*

148. P-38's nearing completion at Burbank. The only large components still to be attached at this point are the propellers. The tricycle-gear undercarriage is just barely visible on the aircraft on the right. The main wheels retracted backward into the tail booms, while the nose wheel retracted backward into an aperture beneath the cockpit. *(Photo: National Air and Space Museum.)*

149

150

151

149. As the P-38 was big for a fighter, with a 52-foot wingspan, there simply wasn't enough room to complete it inside Lockheed's Burbank plant. Thus, final assembly took place outdoors, taking advantage of the mild Southern California weather. As it was worried that the plant would be a prime Japanese target, the roof was eventually camouflaged to look like a small town seen from the air. Almost 50 nearly completed P-38's and Hudsons are visible in this photo. *(Photo: Cradle of Aviation Museum.)*

150. Lockheed, formerly a small Burbank, California, firm, on June 23, 1938, signed a contract with the British Air Ministry for 250 combat-fitted Model 14 aircraft, later named the "Hudson." At the time it was the largest-ever aircraft order to any American manufacturer. Lockheed went on to build 3,000 Hudson bombers and patrol planes through World War II. With the British Hudson orders in hand, Lockheed's work force climbed from 2,500 in December 1938 to 7,000 by the end of 1939. Job-hungry applicants—right from the lean Depression years—flocked to Burbank. By 1945 Lockheed's payroll topped 90,000. Here new British

Hudson bombers, on the left, are reaching final assembly in Lockheed's Burbank plant. The engines and outer wing panels will be attached next. This photo was taken in 1940, before America's entry into the war, as new airliners can still be seen under construction on the right. *(Photo: Cradle of Aviation Museum.)*

151. Completed North American P-51B "Mustang" fuselages on the right have now moved to final assembly and are receiving their wings. The fuselages on the left are having their center and tail sections mated. The Mustang's wings were all-metal two-spar structures built in two panels joined at the fuselage centerline by shear bolts around the periphery of the airfoil. Later-model P-51 wings contained six .50-caliber machine guns as well as provisions for rockets or bombs mounted externally. The P-51 was one of the first fighters to use a thin, high-speed, laminar-flow airfoil, which became standard on most later high-performance fighters. Note how the Mustang had squared off wingtips and tail surfaces, which tended to prevent stalling. *(Photo: National Air and Space Museum.)*

152

153

154

152. P-51D Mustangs in 1944 on North American's Inglewood, California, final assembly line, lacking only propellers and cowling. A major improvement was introduced on the P-51D when a graceful teardrop canopy (bottom, left in the photo) was installed to eliminate a dangerous blind area created by the faired cockpit of earlier versions. The P-51D became the version of Mustang produced in the greatest quantity, 7,954 in all. P-51's were primarily high-altitude, long-range escorts to B-17, B-24 and B-29 bombers, and they scored heavily over German and Japanese interceptors. By the war's end, P-51's had destroyed 4,950 enemy aircraft over Europe, more than any other Air Corps fighter. A total of 14,855 Mustangs (all versions) were built, at a cost of $53,985 each. *(Photo: National Air and Space Museum.)*

153. By the end of 1941, production of the AT-6 trainer was in full swing at North American's Inglewood and Dallas plants alike. The AT-6B, 400 of which were built in 1941 at the Dallas plant, was the same as the AT-6A but equipped with a flexible .30-caliber machine gun in the rear cockpit for gunnery training. The AT-6C, of which 2,970 were built, replaced the aluminum side panels and other components with plywood in an effort to conserve strategic materials. This saved 1,246 pounds of aluminum in each plane. The biggest order was for 4,388 AT-6D's, with the aluminum alloy back in place as well as a new electrical

system. The AT-6B's seen here are just receiving their outer wing panels and now lack only the engine cowling. The landing gear retracted one wheel at a time; this accounts for the one wheel visible on the aircraft being tested in the foreground. *(Photo: National Air and Space Museum.)*

154. The North American B-25 bomber was one of the most famous American planes of World War II, seeing combat on every front. Although originally designed for level bombing from medium altitudes, it was widely used in the Pacific for bombing Japanese targets from treetop level and for strafing and skip-bombing enemy shipping. It was the type used in the famous Doolittle Tokyo raid on April 18, 1942. Able to carry 5,000 pounds of bombs, the B-25 was also the first production bomber to incorporate tricycle landing gear. Later B-25 models had up to eight machine guns or even a 75mm cannon in the nose in order to convert the standard bomber to a powerful ground-attack aircraft. These B-25D's in North American's Inglewood plant are in the final stages of assembly. The two Wright R-2600 engines have been mounted and the wings have been joined outboard of the engine nacelles. The upper turrets, containing two .50-caliber machine guns, have yet to be mounted. Eventually 9,815 B-25's were built at a cost of $106,752 each. *(Photo: National Air and Space Museum.)*

155

155. This view of the Bell plant in Buffalo shows many P-39 fuselages moving down the assembly line and closer to combat. Just visible under the fuselages are floor grooves holding chains, the basis of Bell's moving assembly line. At regular intervals the chains moved the planes forward to another station on the line, where a different group of workmen added the next components. The planes in the center will soon receive their wings. *(Photo: National Air and Space Museum.)*

156

156. P-39's nearing completion at the Bell factory, Buffalo, New York. All major components have been attached and final accessories and cowling are going on. Note the pilot's cabin with its six transparent panels. This cabin was a permanent structure built up as an integral part of the forward fuselage. Directly ahead of the pilot was a windshield panel of laminated shatterproof glass, and armor plate was placed both in front of and behind the pilot. Aluminum doors to the left and right of the pilot had roll-down glass panels much like those on automobile doors. Behind the pilot was a turnover bulkhead of extremely rigid construction capable of withstanding loads in excess of the aircraft's weight. This photo, taken in 1942, shows P-39's still in prewar markings. *(Photo: National Air and Space Museum.)*

157

157. The Martin PBM "Mariner" featured a deep hull with a high "gull" wing in order to lift the engines and propellers above the bow wave and spray. As the Mariners were flying boats, special moving cradles had to be fitted under the fuselage during all factory operations. The PBM fuselages in this 1943 photo have now been fitted with their wing center sections and await installation of tail surfaces, engines, outer wing panels and various subassemblies. The large opening in the nose is for the turret. Aside from the nose turret, the Mariners mounted turrets in the dorsal and tail positions, as well as two flexible guns amidships. Internal stowage was available in each engine nacelle for 4,000 pounds of bombs or depth charges. Early versions of the PBM saw much antisubmarine-patrol service in the Battle of the Atlantic in the early stages of the war. *(Photo: National Air and Space Museum.)*

158. Nearly-complete Martin PBM Mariners fill the "Navy Bay" in the Martin plant near Baltimore. In the early days of World War II, Martin's "Navy Bay" was the largest final-assembly area in the country. Once the completed fuselages reached this area they received their wings, tail and engines. The PBM's wings were all-metal cantilever structures with gull-wing shape. Their entire trailing edge was hinged, the outer section

acting as ailerons, and the inner section as flaps. Tall narrow stabilizer floats were at each wingtip, folding inward on early models and fixed on later models. The wings mounted two Wright R-2600 "Double Cyclone" 14-cylinder engines. The PBM's tail had the same dihedral as the wing's center section, with twin canted fins and rudders. Mariners operated with the U.S. Pacific fleet during the great Naval invasions of the war, such as Iwo Jima and Okinawa, and they provided cover for beachheads at Saipan, Guam and several other notable actions. The Mariner was also the first American aircraft to carry radar equipment on service missions. Martin rolled out a total of 1,200 Mariner flying boats (at a rate of one every two days) between 1940 and 1945. *(Photo: Cradle of Aviation Museum.)*

159. At a late stage of Douglas SBD "Dauntless" production in El Segundo, California, in February 1943, these aircraft have been painted and the wings are about to be mated. By the time of the SBD-4, seen here, production procedures had changed from those for earlier models; the tail surfaces, for instance, were now attached at a later stage. Here, the engine and propeller have just been mounted; the aircraft in the foreground has already had its wings mated. *(Photo: McDonnell Douglas Corp.)*

158

159

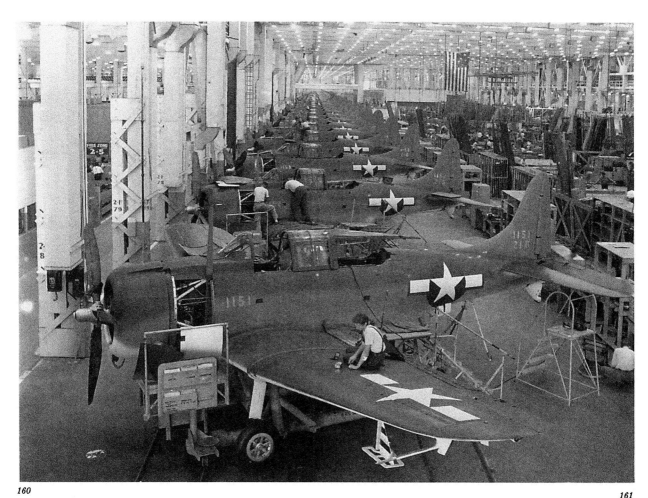

160

161

160. Douglas SBD Dauntlesses in the final stages of assembly. The aircraft's wings had heavy spars in order to withstand dives from 20,000 feet. Perforated dive brakes on the upper and lower surfaces of the outer wing can also be seen. In this view, the cockpit is being completed and the engine cowling is being attached. Note how the propeller blades are enclosed in protective canvas covers. Able to carry up to 1,600 pounds of bombs under the fuselage and 325 pounds under each wing, the Dauntless was particularly effective in the battles of Midway and the Coral Sea. A total of 5,396 were built. *(Photo: Mike Machat.)*

161. The impact of World War II on the Douglas Aircraft Company was phenomenal. Douglas' Santa Monica plant was already bursting at the walls producing A-20's and C-39's, the military version of the DC-2. However, when the Army decided on ordering the upgraded C-47 design there simply wasn't enough room. Thus, the C-47 gave birth to a new factory in Long Beach, California, as well as another one in Oklahoma City. Eventually Long Beach employed 30,000 people. All C-47's were built on a moving production line. Under the fuselages were tracks, along which they moved every few minutes. In this photo the wings are being bolted on and the engine cowlings and propellers added. Altogether, in one configuration or another, there were more than 10,000 C-47's built, at a cost of $85,035 each. C-47's were used in all theaters of the war for hauling food, ammunition and wounded men, for carrying paratroopers and for towing gliders. *(Photo: McDonnell Douglas Corp.)*

162

162. When the U.S. entered World War II, the A-20 "Havoc" high-performance attack bomber was already in large-scale production as a result of foreign orders. Planes were rolling from Douglas production lines at the rate of 18 per day. In fact, Douglas was one of the first companies to institute a moving assembly line. First large-scale production of the A-20B was initiated at a new Douglas plant in Long Beach, as El Segundo was already operating above capacity. The A-20B's seen nearing completion here were very similar to earlier French models, except that they used Wright engines. At this stage engine mating is being completed, with only cowling and propellers still to be attached. *(Photo: National Air and Space Museum.)*

163. New aircraft programs at Douglas' Long Beach and El Segundo plants led in 1941 to the transfer of all A-20 production to the main Douglas factory at Santa Monica, and all A-20 versions after the A-20C were built there. The principal variant produced was the A-20G, seen here in final assembly in 1944. This version was distinguished by a "solid" gun-carrying nose in place of the transparent bomb-aiming position, and was the first attack aircraft to have this feature. The solid nose carried either four 20mm cannons and two machine guns or six .50-caliber machine guns. These aircraft are virtually complete, apparently lacking only propellers and painting. *(Photo: National Air and Space Museum.)*

163

164. When the U.S. entered World War II the Douglas A-20 had already proven its worth in combat flying with British and French Forces. In fact, on July 4, 1942, six A-20's made the first American daylight bombing raid on Europe. The versatile A-20 was used in the Pacific, Middle East, North African, Russian and European theaters. In the Pacific it specialized in dropping parachute bombs on Japanese airfields from low altitudes. A-20's could carry up to 2,000 pounds of bombs externally and 2,000 pounds internally. These A-20G's are being completed outdoors at Douglas' Santa Monica plant, under a camouflaged netting, as there was no more room inside the plant for such final-assembly operations. *(Photo: National Air and Space Museum.)*

164

166

165. Heavily armed and fast, the Douglas A-20 was adapted to some 30 tactical usages, ranging from strafing to low-level skip and torpedo bombing, as well as interception, night flying, observation and smoke laying. In all, 18 models of the A-20 were produced. The efforts of some 42,000 employees at the Santa Monica plant were concentrated on A-20 production until September 1944, when it was superseded by the even faster A-26. More than 7,000 A-20's were built for the U.S. and its allies at a cost of $94,800 each. Here, American and British A-20C's are being completed at the Santa Monica plant. Engine cowling is ready to be attached and some interior work completed. In the rear stands the huge experimental bomber, the XB-19, of which only one was built. Its wing span of 212 feet was the largest to date. Delivered at the end of 1941, the aircraft was used to haul cargo during the war. *(Photo: McDonnell Douglas Corp.)*

166. The Douglas A-26 "Invader," a follow-up to the A-20 Havoc, was the last aircraft produced in the attack category. The heavily armored plane, with its three-man crew, was capable of fast attack operations from low and medium altitudes. Seen here are A-26B's nearing completion at Douglas' Long Beach plant. Note how the aircraft features an "attack" nose, with eight .50-caliber machine guns. Three machine guns were also installed in each wing. It also had upper and lower turrets, both remote-controlled, the upper one able to be locked in the forward firing position for ground attack. The A-26 featured two 2,000-hp Pratt & Whitney R-2800 engines and a thin, high-speed, laminar-flow wing. It first saw combat over Europe in November 1944 and was used for level bombing, ground strafing and rocket attacks over Europe and the Pacific for the remainder of the war. By the war's end 2,502 A-26's had been built at a cost of $185,892 each. *(Photo: McDonnell Douglas Corp.)*

167

167. The Vought F4U "Corsair's" structure was different from those of other World War II fighters in that it made extensive use of large aluminum sheets spot-welded to the metal frame. Each of these sheets was preshaped by stretching it over forms, and some of them incorporated compound curves. Before the sheets were assembled to form larger subassemblies, a stiffening structure was affixed to the inboard side of each sheet. The sheets were then spot-welded to the frame, with remarkably few external fastening seams, resulting in low-drag characteristics. Performance was also enhanced in that the use of spot-welding eliminated the drag caused by rivets, even flush rivets. Much of the wing was also covered in this fashion, with the exception of the center section of the outboard panels, which were fabric-covered. These workers are completing work around the F4U's cockpit area. Early complaints about the Corsair's poor forward visibility prompted a change; thus on the 689th plane a bubble canopy replaced the framed "birdcage" structure then in use, enabling the seat to be raised seven inches. Note the large lowered trailing edge landing flaps, needed to lower the airspeed for carrier landings. *(Photo: National Air and Space Museum.)*

168. A seemingly endless line of Corsairs nears completion at Vought's Stratford, Connecticut, plant. Note how the aircraft's wings folded directly overhead in order to save space on aircraft carriers. The aircraft's landing speed (87 mph) was considered too high for carrier use, however. Its long nose also made observation of the carrier deck difficult. Although the F4U did

pass its carrier-qualification tests, the Navy considered the F4U a land-based fighter, and until the end of 1944 it was solely used in this capacity. The F4U's wing contained six .50-caliber machine guns as well as air scoops located in the center-section leading edge. This scoop took in air for the engine and oil cooler and, with its unique location, did not create extra drag. As with other aircraft, the demand for the F4U far exceeded the production ability of the Vought Company; thus additional assembly lines were set up at Goodyear's Akron and Brewster's Johnsville plants. In all, Vought built 7,830 Corsairs, while Goodyear produced 4,017 and Brewster 735. *(Photo: National Air and Space Museum.)*

169. Final adjustments and accessory installation are being performed on a new B-17F at the Douglas plant in Long Beach, California, in 1943. During the war, results of European combat experiences, especially the requirements for defensive armament, were incorporated into later model B-17's. Earlier .30-caliber armament was replaced by eight .50-caliber guns, two each in top and bottom fuselage power turrets and in a new "stinger" tail turret, and one on each side of the fuselage. Two .30's were retained in the nose. Really large-scale production began with the B-17F, which could be distinguished from the "E" model by a molded plastic nose, seen here. Boeing built 2,300 B-17F's, Douglas 600 and Lockheed 500 in new plants especially built for the purpose. Note the wartime propaganda poster on the nose. *(Photo: McDonnell Douglas Corp.)*

168

169

170

170. A worker installs the platform for the Norden bombsight in the nose of a B-17G in Seattle. The final and most heavily produced version of the B-17 was the "G" model with an added .50-caliber two-gun power turret under the nose, seen here, for defense against direct frontal attack. Boeing built 4,035 G's, Douglas 2,395 and Lockheed 2,250. At the peak of B-17 production in June 1944, the Seattle plant was rolling out 16 planes every 24 hours. *(Photo: National Air and Space Museum.)*

171. The Consolidated B-24D was the most familiar configuration of the "Liberator." Like all Liberators it had distinctive flattened oval engine cowls, which resulted from placing air scoops on each side of the engine. Here, in Ford's Willow Run plant in 1944, basic construction is over and final assembly is taking place. The two basic-construction lines are now merging into one final-assembly line. This line will move until it meets a second, just like it, coming down the plant parallel to it, on the other side of the center partition. Thus Ford had four basic-construction lines and two final-assembly lines. Note the open hinged leading-edge sections, exposing the wing interior. The outer-wing panels have yet to be added to the aircraft at the

rear in the photo. All of these aircraft are still masked for painting. After initial difficulty, the huge Ford plant at Willow Run reached astonishing levels of production, turning out 5,476 of the massive B-24 bombers in 1944–45. In 1944 alone the amount of airframe weight produced at Willow Run (92 million pounds) equaled that of Japan for the entire year and was about half of Germany's. *(Photo: Cradle of Aviation Museum.)*

172. Based on combat experience the B-24 went through a series of major model changes and designations following introduction in 1941 of the mass-produced B-24D. Most of the model changes involved various armament installations, including powered gun turrets in different positions, uprated engine performance, new propellers and turbosuperchargers. The B-24D, seen in final assembly here, was the first model to have an electrically operated Bendix lower gun turret installed. This was supplanted by the Sperry ball turret with twin .50-caliber guns. Remarkably, B-24's shot down 2,600 Axis fighters. This Liberator is now having its eleven-foot-, seven-inch-diameter Hamilton Standard propellers installed. *(Photo: National Air and Space Museum.)*

171

172

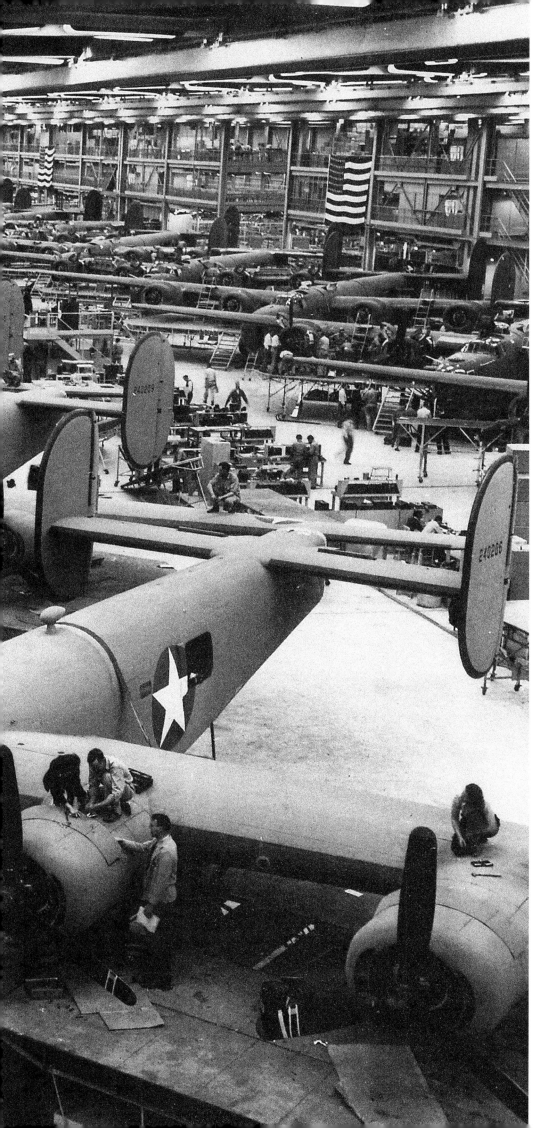

173. A seemingly endless final assembly line of B-24 Liberators at Consolidated's Fort Worth plant. The huge Fort Worth plant—windowless, air-conditioned and 4,000 feet long—swung into operation in March 1942 with two parallel-powered assembly lines—the world's longest. Conducted in monstrous structures such as this, the American method of true mass production was possibly our most significant contribution to the Allied war effort. Consolidated's B-24 assembly lines eliminated the use of stockrooms wherever possible. As storing parts was wasteful, parts and subassemblies moved directly to the final-assembly line. At various stations along the final-assembly line were bays where the parts to be installed on a plane at that particular station were delivered immediately upon fabrication. Note the track underneath these aircraft, which regularly kept them moving toward completion. *(Photo: General Dynamics Corp.)*

174

174. Largest of all the Liberator production models was the B-24J, of which 6,678 were built. It was the only model built by all five Consolidated production facilities: San Diego, Fort Worth, Willow Run, Tulsa and Dallas. Here the last B-24J's are undergoing final assembly in Fort Worth. B-24's had the largest wartime production of any American bomber. They operated on more fronts for a longer period and in a greater number of combat versions than any other bomber. Though their role in Europe was a major one, perhaps the B-24's greatest contribution was in the Pacific. During the peak year of wartime production, 1944, Convair (the result of the 1941 merger of Consolidated and Vultee) outproduced every other aircraft manufacturer in the world. During the war they produced 33,000 aircraft, over ten percent of the nation's total. At peak production during the winter of 1943–44 the Liberator pool (five factories) turned out one B-24 every 55 minutes! Behind the B-24's, in the now largely empty plant shown here, can be seen Convair B-32 "Dominators." The B-32 was first ordered in 1940 at the same time as the B-29 to meet a similar requirement. However, Convair only built 114 B-32's, while 1,588 were cancelled. Fifteen saw limited action in the Western Pacific in 1945. *(Photo: General Dynamics Corp.)*

175.

176

177

175. After successfully lobbying Washington for war work, General Motors undertook the manufacture of both Wildcats and Avengers from Grumman in unused auto plants in New Jersey. GM ran into early production problems, however, as they had never dealt with aircraft construction and its associated problems of critical weight, close tolerances and the use of aircraft aluminum. GM engineers, forced to go to Grumman to study aircraft manufacture in detail, found that their auto-production methods would have to be greatly revised for the production of aircraft. Ultimately, GM's Eastern Aircraft Division produced its first "Wildcat" (FM-1) at Linden in August 1942 and its first "Avenger" (TBM) at Trenton five months later. Production soon mounted in all five GM plants so that by the end of the war Eastern had built 5,920 Wildcats and 7,546 Avengers. To the automotive industry's credit, they all turned out to be excellent airplanes. Here, fuselages near completion on Linden's Wildcat assembly line in 1944. Wing stubs will be attached at the next station. These are FM-2's, which were lighter for improved ability to take off from and land on small carriers. The FM-2 also used the Wright R-1820 engine. A total of 7,815 Wildcats were built by Grumman and GM through August 1945. (Photo: National Air and Space Museum.)

176. Hanging the Hamilton Standard propeller on a nearly complete Grumman F6F "Hellcat." Other workers are completing the engine and accessory hookups. With mass production under way, the Hellcats quickly replaced the Wildcats on the big carriers of the task forces. In the fall of 1943, Bethpage production of the Hellcat was approaching the 100-a-week mark. In one week of November, Grumman produced more planes than it had during the whole of 1940. (Photo: Grumman Corporation.)

177. Grumman's Avenger was the Navy's standard torpedo bomber after the first six months of the war. It was also the largest carrier-based aircraft of World War II. Avengers were successfully used to sink several Japanese aircraft carriers and battleships, as well as bombing land-based targets. Since many men were engaged directly in the war effort, in many cases women produced the weapons of war. Thus Grumman instituted an extensive training program for these new employees, who were given six-week courses, generally at night and in local high schools, with tools and instructors provided by the company. The courses covered basic skills, such as riveting. Following this the new workers were assigned to a small team on the shop floor with an experienced worker to act as an adviser and to give them further practical instruction. These workers are testing the wing-fold mechanism on a completed Avenger to see that it is functioning correctly. (Photo: Grumman Corporation.)

178

178. Previous experience in the production of fighters for the Navy gave Grumman a valuable lead in the development of multiengine fighters for carrier operation. Grumman's twin-engine F7F "Tigercat" was designed to be carrier-based and was destined to become the Navy's first twin to reach mass production and the first carrier-based fighter to have a tricycle undercarriage. Although classified as a fighter, the F7F was also designed to operate in a tactical ground-support role, for which it was heavily armed. The Tigercat was first flown at the end of 1943, when a large order was immediately placed by the Marine Corps, who needed the plane to support land fighting in the Pacific. However, changing requirements made the F7F Tigercat too late for much use in World War II, although many served in Marine units into the Korean War. Here the first of 363 F7F's built is nearing completion in Grumman's experimental shop. The engines and outer wing panels have just been attached and the leading edge, on the sawhorses, will go on next. Note how the landing gear is set into the floor to give clearance for the wings to fold overhead, an arrange-

ment that was new to Grumman. *(Photo: Grumman Corporation.)*

179. BT-13's nearing completion on Vultee's final-assembly line. Visibility from both BT-13 cockpits was good, and wide-set landing gear, clearly seen here, gave it very good ground-handling qualities. These Vultee BT-13's in final assembly are receiving their wings and control surfaces. They now lack only their propellers and cowling. A total of 7,532 BT-13's were built for the Air Corps at a cost of $23,068 each. *(Photo: National Air and Space Museum.)*

180. In Goodyear's final-assembly area in a former Zeppelin hangar in Akron, Ohio, seen here, the control car and the helium-inflated envelope for a Navy K-type airship are being united. The envelope was made of rubberized fabric. Internal supports, known as catenary curtains, held the control car and envelope together. In all, Goodyear built 134 K-type Naval-patrol airships between 1943 and 1945. *(Photo: Cradle of Aviation Museum.)*

181

181. The Piper L-4 "Cub" served on all fronts directing artillery fire and troop movements, delivering messages and transporting officer personnel. Built in Piper's Lock Haven, Pennsylvania, plant, the Cub was built of a welded steel tubing fuselage with aluminum wing ribs and wooden spars. All was covered with cotton fabric, doped and painted. Here at Piper's plant a row of new L-4's nears completion, lacking only the engine cowling. Note the small 65-hp engine with wooden propeller. *(Photo: National Air and Space Museum.)*

182. The Piper L-4 was useful in that it flew safely at low speeds and took off and landed in restricted spaces. Simple and maneuverable, it was used for basic flight instruction, four out of five U.S. pilots in World War II having gotten their original instruction in Piper Cubs. Between 1941 and 1945, 5,673 L-4 Cubs were built for the military at a cost of $2,600 each (the cheapest aircraft of World War II). The total weight of this L-4 is being accurately recorded before the plane finally leaves the Piper factory in 1943. *(Photo: National Air and Space Museum.)*

182

183

184

183. The Sikorsky R-4B "Hoverfly" was the world's first helicopter in regular production and the Air Corps' first service helicopter. The original military model, the XR-4, was developed from the famous experimental VS-300 helicopter. After they first flew in 1942, the Air Corps ordered 30 R-4's for service testing and flight training. They showed such promise that the Air Corps ordered another 100. Several of these can be seen here in various stages of construction at Sikorsky's Bridgeport, Connecticut, plant in 1945. This was the world's first helicopter assembly line. Note the steel tubing of the fuselage on the left, seen covered by fabric on the right. *(Photo: United Technologies Corp.)*

184. At the request of the Air Corps, Beech created an entirely new type of aircraft, the AT-10 twin-engine advanced pilot trainer. In it at least 50 percent of the Army's multiengine pilots received their transitional training. Designed at a time when aluminum was scarce, the AT-10 was constructed entirely of plywood, except for the cowlings and cockpit enclosure. Some of the 1,771 AT-10's built can be seen here nearing final assembly. These fuselages are awaiting attachment of wings and engines. Note the dullness of the wood compared to the shininess of aluminum AT-11 fuselages (see photo 29, above). *(Photo: National Air and Space Museum.)*

185

186

187

185. Beech's C-45 "Expeditor" was the military-transport version of the commercial Beech Model 18. Virtually complete in their wartime colors, the C-45's lined up here represent some of the 7,400 aircraft built by Beech for the armed forces during the War. All were built in Wichita. Training-plane production was halted in March 1944, however, so floor space and personnel could be freed for the production of subassemblies of combat aircraft. *(Photo: National Air and Space Museum.)*

186. The main assembly area of Republic's Farmingdale, Long Island, New York, plant, seen during a break in 1943. These early P-47D razorback Thunderbolts are nearing final assembly. Of the completed fuselages lining the right side, only the first one has its tail assembly attached. Wings, stored at the far right

(not seen in the photo), were mated to the fuselages in the two lines down the center. Cowling and propellers went on last. Note how workers were urged to "Keep That Line Rolling!" By the end of 1943, P-47 production had reached its peak of 660 aircraft per month. Throughout the following year the *daily* average would be maintained at over 20—almost one P-47 per hour! *(Photo: Cradle of Aviation Museum.)*

187. Late-model P-47D Thunderbolts in Republic's final assembly area, in 1944. These later models being built for the U.S. and England were equipped with a "bubble" canopy to provide better all-around visibility. The two lines in the center will next receive their cowling, propeller and canopy. *(Photo: Cradle of Aviation Museum.)*

188

188. In the spring of 1942, the War Production Board began to seek a second source for Thunderbolts, not just to increase production but also to ensure that there were factories situated away from the coast and apparent vulnerability. Thus a new site was selected in Evansville, Indiana, in a farmer's field adjacent to the city's municipal airport. On September 19, 1942, just five months after ground was first broken for the new factory, the first P-47 rolled off its assembly line. The first Indiana-built P-47 was appropriately named *Hoosier Spirit,* and this division consistently produced P-47's ahead of schedule. Here a new P-47D is nearly set to roll out the Evansville factory door. Oil is being added to the engine prior to its first runup. *(Photo: Jim Boss.)*

189. A view of the huge balloon room at the plant of the Firestone Tire and Rubber Company in Akron, Ohio, where as many as twelve large "barrage" balloons could be assembled and inflated at one time. Barrage balloons were widely used by America and Britain during the war. Great numbers of these captive balloons were let up on long steel cables over cities and invasion fleets to keep enemy planes from flying low enough for accurate bombing. The heavy steel cables that anchored them could sever the wing of a low-flying aircraft. Firestone produced the balloons for the U.S. and its allies. In this photo, workers in the foreground are assembling a gas bag out of a silver rubberized fabric. The balloons in the rear, inflated with helium, have passed inspection. *(Photo: Cradle of Aviation Museum.)*

190. In December 1943 it was decided not to use the B-29 "Superfortress" in the European Theater, thereby permitting the plane to be sent to the Pacific, where its great range made it particularly suited for the long over-water flight required to attack the Japanese homeland. During the last two months of 1944, B-29's began operating against Japan from the islands of Saipan, Guam and Tinian. After the February 1945 capture of Iwo Jima, an island nearly midway between Saipan and Japan, fighter escorts became available to the B-29's. However, the Iwo Jima–based fighters virtually put themselves out of business by eliminating most of the defending fighters, and the B-29's roamed at will all over Japan to the point where they would drop leaflets on selected cities, warning the population to leave before the scheduled attack. As enemy-fighter opposition diminished toward the end of World War II it was possible to improve the speed and bomb load of the B-29 by deleting all the gun turrets and sighting blisters. The guns were no longer needed, as the few enemy fighters left could be dealt with by the American fighter escorts. Thus all the B-29B's, like those seen here under construction at Martin in 1945, are notable for their lack of armament. Note the absence of turrets on the upper fuselage. World War II was eventually brought to an end, without the necessity of an invasion of Japan, by two B-29's that had a greater impact on world history than any aircraft previously: the B-29's that dropped the first atomic bombs on Hiroshima and Nagasaki. Altogether, 3,970 Superfortresses were built: 2,766 by Boeing, 668 by Bell and 536 by Martin, at a cost of $619,000 each, making the B-29 the most expensive American aircraft of World War II. *(Photo: National Air and Space Museum.)*

189

190

Rollouts

191

191. When the Japanese attacked Pearl Harbor on December 7, 1941, both the Navy and Marines were flying the Brewster F2A "Buffalo" fighter. F2A's were swiftly removed from frontline American service, however, after a disastrous encounter with the Japanese over Midway. This was not so much the fault of the F2A; rather, the Japanese pilots were more experienced, and their "Zero" was a vastly superior fighter. Under different circumstances, where the Buffalo was not overwhelmed by sheer numbers, it proved to be an effective fighter. Buffalos were successfully flown by Finland against the Soviet Union for three years in the 1940's, shooting down Soviet "Spitfires" on more than one occasion. When production of the Buffalo was concluded, 162 had been delivered to the Navy and an additional 346 export models had been built. Since space at Brewster's Long Island City plant was incredibly tight, all final assembly and testing of F2A's took place on Long Island's Roosevelt Field. This early F2A, still without paint, stands before a Roosevelt Field hangar in 1940 in a situation typical of these operations. This was an extraordinarily inefficient way to run an aircraft plant. *(Photo: Cradle of Aviation Museum.)*

192. One of the least successful combat aircraft put into production in America during the war was the Brewster SB2A "Buccaneer." A backup design to the Curtiss "Helldiver," the SB2A first flew in 1941. Brewster's scattering of buildings around Long Island City and Newark was clearly inadequate for the new production task, and building more plants on Long Island was ruled out by the War Production Board (there were already too many "targets" there), so Brewster set up a new plant in Johnsville, Pennsylvania. The SB2A suffered from design and production problems, however, and, of the 771 built for the U.S. and England, none ever saw combat. Here the prototype SB2A is being readied for a flight test at Newark in 1941. Note the turret in mockup form, which was discarded on all production models. *(Photo: Jim Maas.)*

193. On the apron outside the final-assembly department in Buffalo, a Curtiss P-40D receives its final engine tests and adjustments before being turned over to the flight-test department. The aircraft's compass is also being "swung" (calibrated) on the "compass rose" beneath it. Visible under the propeller is the bulge housing the oil and glycol radiators. The three-radiator cluster was fully enclosed in a huge streamlined housing beneath the fuselage, opening into a large air scoop at the forward end. This early-1942 photograph reveals many near-complete P-40's, one O-52 and a factory being repainted. *(Photo: Cradle of Aviation Museum.)*

192

193

194

195

194. Fifteen new Curtiss P-40E's are lined up in a "V-for-victory" formation in Buffalo prior to delivery to the Air Corps. As the war progressed, however, it became obvious that the P-40 was definitely second-rate equipment. By April 1944 the inventory of P-40's with the Air Corps numbered 2,499. P-40's were now being assigned only to low-priority areas—they had simply been in production too long. As late as the summer of 1944, however, P-40's were still being ordered in quantity. In December 1944 the last P-40 rolled off Curtiss' production line. *(Photo: Cradle of Aviation Museum.)*

195. Another C-46 "Commando" rolls out of the Curtiss plant in Buffalo. Because of their greater load-carrying ability and better performance at high altitude, compared with the C-47, C-46's were assigned primarily to the Pacific. C-46's almost single-handedly kept China in the war after the fall of Burma in 1942 by flying war material over the "Hump"—that is, over the Himalayas and into China. All told Curtiss built 3,144 C-46's at Buffalo and St. Louis at a cost of $224,550 each. *(Photo: Cradle of Aviation Museum.)*

196. Curtiss built a total of 978 SB2C-1 "Helldivers" for the Navy, as well as 900 for the Army, known as the

A-25. This was followed with the uprated SB2C-3, of which 1,112 were built. These were followed by 2,045 SB2C-4's, which featured underwing attach points for bombs and rockets. Throughout 1944, Helldivers gradually supplanted the older Douglas SBD dive-bombers in the final American drive across the Pacific. This completed SB2C-3 rolls out of Curtiss' Columbus, Ohio, plant. *(Photo: National Air and Space Museum.)*

197. By 1940 the Navy began to develop smaller escort carriers (CVE's), which, being smaller, also had less room to store aircraft. Since early Wildcats had fixed wings, it took Grumman ingenuity and engineering skill to develop the folding-wing version of the Wildcat. Folding the wings vertically would have made the aircraft very tall and unstable; thus Grumman attached the folding outer portions of the wing with skewed-axis hinges, so they could pivot around to the rear while simultaneously rotating to be stowed leading-edge-down. The 163rd F4F-3 was fitted with folding wings of this kind. Here, in 1941, the wings' advantage is emphasized in a "five-into-two" demonstration using the new Wildcats. Now many more Wildcats could be fitted on aircraft carriers. The new wings also added $5,000 to the $26,000 cost of the F4F. *(Photo: Cradle of Aviation Museum.)*

197

196

198

199

200

198. These new Hellcats in Bethpage, awaiting fly-away delivery by Navy pilots, became the backbone of Naval-fighter forces in World War II. By the end of the war, the F6F had destroyed a confirmed 5,155 enemy aircraft, out of the U.S. Navy's total carrier-based score of 6,477. In doing so the Hellcat established a 19-1 "kill ratio." This is remarkable in that the Hellcat was in action for less than two years. But Grumman had built over 12,000 of them in just 30 months in 1943-45. In fact, in the single month of March 1945, Grumman's 22,100 employees turned out 664 military aircraft—often at the rate of one an hour! This is an aircraft-production record that still stands. In all, 12,275 Hellcats were built by Grumman, at a cost of $72,000 each. *(Photo: Cradle of Aviation Museum.)*

199. Although a 1933 design, the Grumman J2F "Duck" amphibian remained in production throughout the war, and was successfully used by the Navy, Air Corps and Coast Guard for observation, transport, utility and rescue work. These were the only biplanes operated in combat areas by the Armed Forces throughout the war. Grumman built almost 300 Ducks in nine different versions. However, in order to free up Grumman for fighter production, further Duck pro-duction was contracted out to the Columbia Aircraft Company of Valley Stream, Long Island, New York. The Duck had an aluminum fuselage and aluminum-frame wings, fabric-covered. Here four new Ducks, of the 330 Columbia built, are run up outside their suburban plant in 1944. *(Photo: Valley Stream Historical Society.)*

200. In January 1939, the first three "Bombers for Britain" came off Lockheed's assembly line, as seen here. By June, however, only 48 of these Hudsons had been completed, and there was some doubt that the company would meet the December deadline of 250 planes. However, Lockheed then took a step unprecedented in the highly competitive airframe industry, and, in a bold move, subcontracted a substantial amount of parts for the bombers to Rohr Aircraft in San Diego. Production soon began to increase rapidly, and the 250th plane rolled out of the factory seven weeks ahead of schedule. Soon, even larger orders from the British followed. Lockheed thus became the first American aircraft company to introduce mass subcontracting. All others soon followed suit. *(Photo: Cradle of Aviation Museum.)*

201

202

203

201. A group of new Lockheed P-38 "Lightnings" lined up at the Burbank plant in early 1942, ready for delivery to the Army Air Corps. The Lightning first went into large-scale war operations late in 1942 during the North African campaign, where the Germans named it "the fork-tailed devil." Equipped with external fuel tanks, the P-38 was extensively used as a long-range escort fighter, and it saw action in both the European and Pacific combat theaters. It was also used for dive bombing, level bombing, ground strafing and photo reconnaissance. By the end of the war, 9,923 P-38's had been built in some 18 models, at a cost of $107,147 each. *(Photo: Cradle of Aviation Museum.)*

202. Towing a completed late model P-47D from Republic's factory to the flight line for testing, in 1944. During that year, Republic became the largest producer of any single type of fighter aircraft in the world. *(Photo: Cradle of Aviation Museum.)*

203. New P-47's lined up outside Republic's Long Island factory. From 5,900 employees in 1941, by the end of 1944 Republic had expanded its work force to 24,450, and its two plants together produced 5,200 planes in that one year. Republic had also steadily cut the man-hours required to produce a single plane from an average of 22,925 for the first 773 planes to 6,290 for the 10,000th. *(Photo: Cradle of Aviation Museum.)*

204. A new B-17F rolls out of the Vega Aircraft plant in Burbank. In 1938 the Vega Aircraft Corporation, a Lockheed subsidiary formed in 1937, bought 30 acres next to Union Air Terminal and began building a plant to build Ventura bombers for Britain. Vega later became the first to make deliveries of these heavy bombers under a pooled-facilities agreement with two other aircraft manufacturers. Vega merged with Lockheed in 1943 and began to produce Boeing B-17's under license. *(Photo: Cradle of Aviation Museum.)*

204

205

206

208

207

205. The heart of the B-17's performance was the 1,000-hp Wright Cyclone engine—one of the most dependable power plants ever built. This new Vega-built LB-17 is having all four of its new engines tested simultaneously, in 1943. Most bombers were delivered, saw combat and, often, were destroyed within a few weeks of construction. The first B-17 raids on Europe occurred in July 1942. *(Photo: Cradle of Aviation Museum.)*

206. Three more shiny new AT-6's roll out of North American's Inglewood, California, plant. The AT-6 advanced trainer was one of the most widely used aircraft in history. It was used by both the U.S. Air Corps and Navy, as well as by the air forces of 30 allied nations. Many British pilots in the Battle of Britain were trained in Canada on "Harvards," the Canadian version of the AT-6. These AT-6's are receiving their final cleaning; on one, the cowling is ready to be installed over the Pratt & Whitney R-1340 engine. A total of 15,495 AT-6's and SNJ's (the Navy version) were built at a cost of $24,952 each. *(Photo: National Air and Space Museum.)*

207. A P-39 Airacobra rollout at Bell's Buffalo plant. P-39's had a major drawback, being built without superchargers. As newer and heavier models of the P-39 were produced, performance of the plane fell without the extra power of a supercharged engine. The Airacobra could no longer be considered suitable as an interceptor, or successfully engage in dogfights, since it was outclassed by newer, lighter, more maneuverable Axis fighters. The P-39's Allison V-1710 engine really only gave good performance below 10,000 feet. Thus, by the end of 1941, the fighter was reclassed in a ground-attack role. Note the cannon shaft through the propeller hub, and engine exhausts behind the cockpit. Inside the plant, both British and American P-39's near completion. *(Photo: Cradle of Aviation Museum.)*

208. A lineup of new P-39's awaiting delivery outside the Bell plant. The P-39 saw extensive combat throughout the world during World War II, especially on the South Pacific, Mediterranean and Russian fronts. When Airacobra production ended in 1944, Bell had built 9,584 P-39's at a cost of $48,600 each. A total of 4,773 P-39's were sent to the Soviet Union, where the Russian pilots liked the plane for its ground-attack capability. It was also used by the Free French and British forces. *(Photo: Cradle of Aviation Museum.)*

209

211

209. Designed in the late 1930's, the Martin JRM "Mars" was the largest flying boat in the world when built. Originally designed for the Navy as a long-range bomber, the JRM was used during the war as a long-range transport between California and Hawaii. Here the first Mars is being moved from one Martin assembly building to another. As the aircraft was a flying boat, the wheels seen here are simply beaching gear for moving the aircraft. The pairs of wheels were fitted onto the hull separately. The Mars was first flown in 1942. Only five were built. Note the new B-26's dwarfed in the background. *(Photo: Cradle of Aviation Museum.)*

210. This rear view of a brand new Northrop P-61 "Black Widow" reveals the aircraft's unique structural layout. Two tail booms extend aft from the two engine nacelles to the vertical-stabilizer assemblies. The tail unit included the horizontal stabilizer and elevator, two vertical stabilizers, which were faired into the tail booms, and two rudders. The horizontal and vertical stabilizers were of all-metal construction, with a single-piece elevator and aerodynamically balanced rudders. The P-61 was powered by two 2,000-hp Pratt & Whitney R-2800 engines, each driving a four-bladed propeller. Also visible here is the rear Plexiglas enclosure for the gunner. *(Photo: Cradle of Aviation Museum.)*

210

211. These nearly complete P-61 Black Widows are receiving their engine cowlings and other accessories prior to flight-testing at Northrop's Hawthorne, California, plant. The P-61's unusual ailerons consisted of four retractable aileron panels, all mechanically connected to the control system. The retractable panels were perforated metal scoop-shaped strips which, when raised, spoiled the airflow and reduced lift on one wing. Because of the full-span landing flaps, which ran almost the whole length of the outer wing panels, the ailerons were necessarily small in area. They mainly served only to give "feel" to the aileron operation. P-61's first reached combat zones in Europe and the Pacific in mid-1944. Most were painted a glossy black to blend into the night sky, hence the name "Black Widow." The most expensive American fighter of World War II, a total of 700 P-61's were built at a cost of $170,000 each. *(Photo: National Air and Space Museum.)*

212. All new production aircraft were extensively tested before they were shipped to the front. Here, fresh off the assembly line, a Douglas A-20 is being test-flown in Santa Monica. In this particular case the test pilot is probably more famous than the aircraft. The famous Douglas "Wrong Way" Corrigan worked as a test pilot for Douglas during World War II. He is better known as the pilot who flew from Long Island to Ireland in 1938 and then announced he must have flown the wrong way because he meant to fly to Los Angeles! *(Photo: Cradle of Aviation Museum.)*

212

213

213. The Vought "Kingfisher" incorporated some revolutionary structural techniques, including spot welding. It was based upon the Vought Company's considerable experience of observation aircraft and was designed to replace earlier Vought biplanes in a similar role. Generally, the Kingfishers were catapult-launched and employed a large central float under the fuselage. They were, however, delivered in the land-plane configuration seen here. This is the OS2U-3 model, which was equipped with extra fuel tanks and more armor protection. Starting in 1941, Vought delivered 1,006 OS2U-3's before production ended in 1942. This Kingfisher, on the ramp outside the Vought-Sikorsky Stratford plant, is having its compass calibrated on a "compass rose." *(Photo: Cradle of Aviation Museum.)*

214. A new barrage balloon is being test-inflated at the General Tire & Rubber Company plant in Ohio. This is an English-type balloon that was used successfully over London and other English cities to deter low-flying German aircraft. It was different from previous balloons turned out in Akron in that it had three fins instead of four. After passing inspection, the balloon would be deflated, packed and shipped to the front. It would then be attached to a heavy steel cable anchored to a winch. *(Photo: Cradle of Aviation Museum.)*

215. During 1944 and 1945, while producing P-47's, Republic on Long Island was also heavily involved in producing JB-2 jet bombs for the Army. Essentially an exact duplicate of a captured German V-1, the JB-2 gave America its first experience in guided-missile production and operation. As they realized that guided missiles would be the weapons of the future, the Air Corps awarded Republic the JB-2 airframe contract and Ford the contract to reproduce the German Argus pulse jet engine. Within 60 days Republic produced its first JB-2. Made almost entirely of welded steel, JB-2's were produced in large numbers for the invasion of Japan. The American JB-2's were intended to be launched from ships and aircraft in the invasion. Although they were never actually used in combat, many were test-launched successfully and provided valuable experience. (This view dates from 1945.) *(Photo: Cradle of Aviation Museum.)*

214

215

216

216. The end of World War II also saw the beginning of the end of the propeller-driven fighter. When German jets first appeared in the skies over Europe, the Air Corps responded by organizing a crash jet-plane program. Early contractors in the program were Bell, Lockheed and Republic. At first Republic was asked to produce a jet-engine version of the P-47. They deemed this impractical, however, and instead produced the 600-mph P-84 "Thunderjet" design. The P-84 had the jet engine in its middle and the intake in its nose—the first jet with a nose intake—because its GE axial-flow engine required more air. In 1945, as World War II was winding down, Republic completed its first highly streamlined XP-84 in Farmingdale, seen here soon afterward, in 1946. The canopy and tail clearly resemble those of a P-47. The Jet Age had begun. *(Photo: Cradle of Aviation Museum.)*

Morale Builders

217. Since most aircraft workers performed tedious, repetitive tasks, several unique morale-boosting programs were instituted. These music, sports, entertainment and awards programs helped create a level of camaraderie and morale among workers that has probably never been surpassed. Such programs are rare today. Often musical groups would entertain workers during lunch-hour breaks to provide some needed relief. In a typical instance seen here, the McFarland Twins have just been serenading workers at the Dade Brothers glider plant in Mineola, New York. Company President George Dade, in the middle, is reading reports of CG-4 glider activity in Europe. *(Photo: George Dade.)*

218. To make workers feel more like part of a unified endeavor, corporate presidents and high-ranking executives would often mingle with or address assemblies of the employees. Such talks might include reports of the latest production figures, discussions of any problems, and, especially interesting, news of how the company's products were performing on the front. Jake Swirbul, Chief of Production at Grumman, would tour the plants and talk to the plane makers almost daily, making them feel he was one of them. Here, Swirbul rallies workers at Grumman's Bethpage plant. Two incomplete G-21 "Gooses" flank the ceremony. *(Photo: Grumman Corporation.)*

217

218

219

219. One of the best ways of increasing workers' satisfaction with their jobs was to have returning war heroes visit the factories that built their aircraft. Both the Air Corps and Navy promoted this practice. The heroes would praise the workers for their skill and dedication and ask them to sustain their efforts. For example, in early 1942, Navy Lt. Butch O'Hare (center) visited Grumman on Long Island shortly after becoming the first American Navy Ace of World War II. Flying a Grumman F4F Wildcat, O'Hare shot down five Japanese "Sally" bombers attacking the U.S.S. *Lexington* in February 1942. Proud Wildcat builders pose beside him. *(Photo: Grumman Corporation.)*

220. In an effort to recognize companies for fulfilling all their production quotas, the Army/Navy "E" award (for "Excellence"), given in the form of a flag, was instituted. Hundreds of these awards were given to large and small companies throughout the war in a further effort to boost workers' morale. The first Navy "E" awarded to an aircraft manufacturer was given to Grumman on April 16, 1942. Thousands of employees gathered in front of the main plant as several Naval dignitaries, seen here, presented the award and praised the company for its production of Wildcats. Note the brand new Wildcat in the foreground and the Navy "E" flag flying. *(Photo: Grumman Corporation.)*

221. All companies large and small contributed to the war effort, and even the smallest were recognized for excellence in production. Here, the Agawam Aircraft Company of Sag Harbor, Long Island, New York, with less than 200 employees, receives its "E"-award flag. Agawam was a subcontractor to Grumman. *(Photo: Cradle of Aviation Museum.)*

222. Politicians too, made a point of visiting aircraft-production plants. Joseph Grew (right), U.S. Ambassador to Japan until December 7, 1941, and Edsel Ford inspect a big B-24 Liberator built by Ford at their Willow Run, Michigan, plant. This was during a tour of the war plants in the Detroit area in February 1943. *(Photo: Cradle of Aviation Museum.)*

220

222

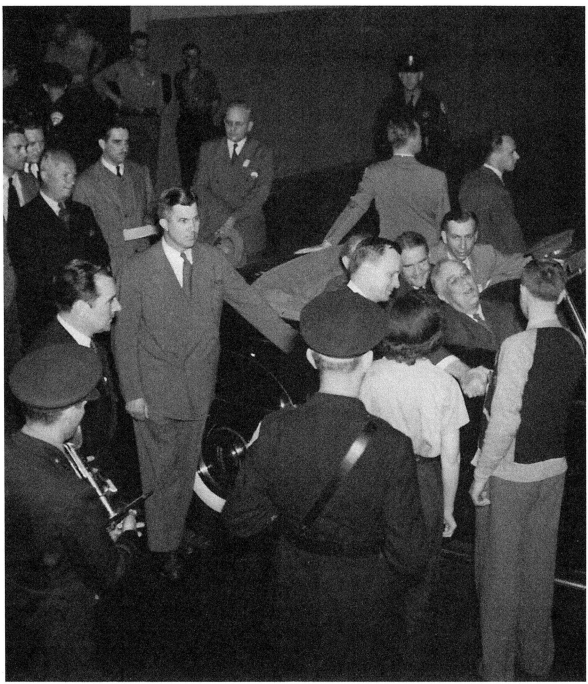

223

223. In May 1943, the doors at Republic's Evansville, Indiana, plant swung open, and, to workers' surprise and delight, President Franklin Roosevelt rolled through for a tour. In the car with him in this photo are Mundy Peale and Ralph Damon, President of Republic. Republic's Evansville plant produced only P-47 Thunderbolts. Such impromptu tours, with the President praising the workers' efforts, no doubt did much to increase their morale. *(Photo: Cradle of Aviation Museum.)*

224. Grumman, like other manufacturers, realized that its workers needed diversion to lighten the load of a tedious day, and, sometimes, help with their personal problems. Management arranged for live music to fill the cafeterias during mealtimes, ran three nurseries for the children of their woman workers (Grumman was among the first companies to do so) and provided professional counseling services. An extensive sports program was set up, and, during lunch breaks and afternoon rest periods, the fields around the plants resembled a minor Olympics. This photo shows one of several women's softball teams that played teams of other Long Island defense contractors. *(Photo: Cradle of Aviation Museum.)*

225. A lunch-hour softball game alongside an active runway at Grumman. New Hellcats and Avengers can be seen in the rear. *(Photo: Cradle of Aviation Museum.)*

224

225

226

226. Grumman's Hellcat assembly line takes a break for ping-pong on the shop floor. *(Photo: Cradle of Aviation Museum.)*

Milestone Aircraft

227. If an organization had enough money they could, through the purchase of War Bonds, buy an aircraft and donate it to the war effort. Manufacturers could also sponsor planes through voluntary payroll deductions. Sponsorship of a fighter cost $75,000; a bomber cost up to $300,000. Through such plans the government raised a total of over $550 million, which paid for thousands of individual planes. Wherever possible, the Air Corps marked the plane with an appropriate inscription, as was done with this B-17F, which carried the sponsoring company's name. B-17F's made the first attack of the war against Germany in January 1943 with a raid on Wilhelmshaven. Later raids on Schweinfurt and other industrial targets resulted in losses of up to 60 planes per mission. Losses decreased greatly with increased fighter protection and improved B-17 models. *(Photo: National Air and Space Museum.)*

227

228. The 5,000th B-17 built by Boeing since Pearl Harbor is seen here after having been rolled out of Boeing's Seattle plant. Every worker from various fabrication shops and subassembly areas wrote his or her name on this B-17G. Making an exception to its usual practice, the Air Corps accepted the plane with its unofficial markings. *Five Grand* later completed 78 missions with the 96th Bomb Group. Growing production efficiency allowed the man-hours needed to produce a B-17 to drop from 55,000 in 1941 to 19,000 in 1944. Eventually the availability of the instruments of destruction would be the deciding element in World War II. Here, Boeing was a major factor. *(Photo: National Air and Space Museum.)*

229

229. The last of 6,981 B-17's built in Seattle was this B-17G, covered with the names of targets for the rollout ceremony on April 9, 1945. It was paired with a new B-29A built in nearby Renton and marked with a Tokyo banner to signify the change of emphasis in the war effort. The B-17G, like the "F," was built in three factories, 4,035 by Boeing in Seattle, 2,395 by Douglas in Long Beach and 2,250 by Lockheed at Burbank, and was used almost exclusively in Europe from the end of 1943 onwards. One of the most famous American airplanes ever built, the B-17 (in its various versions) was used in every combat zone of World War II, particularly for strategic daylight bombing of German industrial targets. By the time B-17 production was halted in May 1945, a total of 12,726 had been built at a cost of $223,742 each. *(Photo: National Air and Space Museum.)*

230. This Republic P-47D was also paid for by War Bonds purchased by employees through a voluntary payroll deduction. It was the 18th such Thunderbolt paid for by Republic workers. The turbosupercharger area is clearly visible here. *(Photo: Cradle of Aviation Museum.)*

231. With suitable ceremonies, the 5,000th P-47 Thunderbolt has just rolled off Republic's Farmingdale assembly line. The P-47 had gone as far as Model "N" and was still undergoing refinement and in quantity production, when the war ended. *(Photo: Cradle of Aviation Museum.)*

230

231

232

233

232. At the end of 1944 Republic's two factories were producing 28 P-47's per day, and the backlog of unfilled orders stood at $475 million. By September 1944, the 10,000th P-47 had been completed. Jacqueline Cochran, then chief of the WASP Ferry pilot service, christened it *Ten Grand. Ten Grand* is seen here with its pilot, Col. Gladwyn Pinkston (right); it served with the 12th Air Force in Italy. *(Photo: Cradle of Aviation Museum.)*

233. By July 1945, *Fifteen Grand*, seen here, rolled off the assembly line, marking the production of 5,000 P-47's in the ten months since *Ten Grand* had been

completed. In addition to establishing an impressive record as a high-altitude bomber escort, the P-47 Thunderbolt was widely used as a low-altitude fighter-bomber because of its ability to absorb battle damage and keep flying. By the end of the war, the P-47 had been used in every active war theater, with the exception of Alaska. In addition to serving with the U.S. Air Corps, P-47's were flown in action by the British, Free French, Russians and Brazilians. In total some 15,683 P-47's were built, at a cost of $93,000 each, making this the most heavily produced type of all American fighter aircraft. *(Photo: Cradle of Aviation Museum.)*

235

234.   The 2,000th aircraft produced by Curtiss's "2B" plant in Buffalo, this C-46 Commando was also the "Blood Bank Special." In an effort to boost contributions, employees were allowed to write their names on this plane if they donated blood for the war effort. *(Photo: National Air and Space Museum.)*

235.   This group photo taken in 1944 at the Dade Brothers factory, Mineola, New York, shows plant staff posing with the 100th spruce-and-mahogany Waco CG-4 glider wing produced. Eventually Dade built nearly 1,000 of the 83-foot-long wings. Note the unusually high percentage of women workers. Dade's plant was located about one mile from where Lindbergh had taken off for Paris. *(Photo: George Dade.)*

236.   The 10,000th Curtiss P-40 "Warhawk" built is being noted as such in Buffalo, in this photo. This is an "L" model, with more firepower and improved radio and carburetor. Although the P-40 was not the best of American fighters, it is necessary to examine the quantity of Air Corps fighters produced throughout the critical early war years in order to understand the P-40's true worth (see also next photo). In 1941, 2,246 P-40's were built and only 926 P-39's and 609 fighters of other types. In 1942 production of P-40's was up to 4,453 compared with 1,972 P-39's, 1,264 P-38's, 632 P-51's and 530 P-47's. *(Photo: National Air and Space Museum.)*

236

237

238

237. The Curtiss P-40 Warhawk served in numerous combat areas: the Aleutian Islands, Italy, the Middle East, the Far East and the Southwest Pacific. Many were even sent to Russia. Although often outclassed by its adversaries in speed, maneuverability and rate of climb, the P-40 earned a reputation for ruggedness in battle. This P-40, going through flight testing in Buffalo, is emblazoned with the insignia of all the 28 Air Forces with which the plane served in the war. Ultimately, 13,737 P-40's were produced, at a cost of $44,892 each. *(Photo: Cradle of Aviation Museum.)*

238. In March 1943, at New York's La Guardia Airport, Brigadier General Willis Taylor (right) looks on as actress Elisabeth Bergner christens a brand new P-40 as the *Loyalty*. Taylor was Commanding General of the First Fighter Command stationed at nearby Mitchel Field. This fighter was a gift to the Army Air Corps by the Loyalty Committee, an organization representing 16,000 refugees from Nazi oppression. *(Photo: Cradle of Aviation Museum.)*

239. The 10,000th fighter built by Bell Aircraft in Buffalo, New York, is seen here. The vast majority of these fighters were P-39 Airacobras, but this particular plane is a P-63 Kingcobra. Developed from the P-39, the P-63 had a more powerful engine and a laminarflow wing. The Army Air Forces never used the P-63 in combat, although some were used as fighter trainers. A total of 3,305 P-63's were built, of which 2,456 were sent to the Soviet Union. The P-63 had good low-altitude performance and was widely used by the Soviets as a "tank buster." *(Photo: National Air and Space Museum.)*

239

240. The last B-24 Liberator built by Consolidated in Fort Worth, the 3,034th, nears completion in the now largely empty Consolidated plant, December 12, 1944. Note that the aircraft has been signed by all production workers. At peak production in Fort Worth, 30,000 workers toiled around the clock to build a new B-24 every four hours. The B-24 was employed in every combat theater during the war, dropping an impressive total of 634,831 tons of bombs during 312,734 missions. It was particularly suited for long-range missions. A total of 18,481 Liberators were produced, at a cost of $295,516 each. *(Photo: General Dynamics Corp.)*

241

243

241. A happy group of Grumman employees gathers around the right wing stub of the last F4F they built, in January 1943. In wartime tradition, the last aircraft has been signed by everyone who worked on it. Wildcat production was being shifted to General Motors at this time in order to free up Grumman for F6F Hellcat production. Grumman built three times as many planes in 1942 as they had in the whole 12 years of the company's history. *(Photo: Grumman Corporation.)*

242. The 10,000th Hellcat, an F6F-5, seen here, was delivered to VBF-87 aboard the USS *Ticonderoga* in May of 1945. In all, the Hellcat production line ran over three years and produced over 12,000 Hellcats, the most aircraft of any one type ever to emerge from a single production source. *(Photo: Grumman Aerospace Corp.)*

243. On V-E Day, May 8, 1945, Grumman employees in the Hellcat shop await President Truman's speech. Note the mix of older men and younger women. By the end of the war the American work force had also become truly integrated for the first time, as can be seen here. Of course, with the end of the war, the vast majority of the employees in this photo were immediately laid off. Grumman had an amazing wartime production record, and met or surpassed its production quota every month. During World War II, 34,664 Grumman-designed military planes were built for the U.S. and Allied fighting forces. (Grumman built 18,868 of these, General Motors 15,466 and Columbia 330.) Altogether this is about 13 percent of the total number of warplanes built—springing from just one company! *(Photo: Grumman Corporation.)*

Shipping

244. The war in Europe brought new orders to Grumman on Long Island. France ordered 100 F4F-3's in 1940. Unfortunately, France fell before the planes were delivered, and they were diverted to the British, who renamed the F4F the "Martlet." The major difference between these and American F4F's was the substitution of a Wright engine for the Pratt & Whitney. The British F4F's were the first Grumman planes to see combat. Grumman's F4F was also essentially the U.S. Navy's only operational fighter until the end of August 1943, when Grumman's F6F went into action. These completed British F4F's are awaiting shipping from Long Island's Roosevelt Field, not far from Grumman's plant, in 1941. *(Photo: Cradle of Aviation Museum.)*

245. World War II aircraft, once completed, had to be shipped to the front by one means or another. By far the largest aircraft shipper during the war was Dade Brothers, of Mineola, Long Island, New York. In the prewar years Dade was a house builder and trucker of wrecked aircraft. By 1940 the Dade interests, talents and experience had been merged into the Dade Brothers shipping business. By the war's end, Dade had established 13 aircraft packing and shipping centers at various points around the country. Normally, aircraft were disassembled, sprayed with anticorrosion compound and placed in specially engineered crates. These crates were so designed that the weight of the plane was carried on only those points that would carry it on the ground. The aircraft rode on flexible fittings so that bends in the crate were not transmitted to the airframe. Here a Brewster F2A is seen in the middle of processing at Roosevelt Field, Garden City, Long Island, New York, in 1941. *(Photo: George Dade.)*

246. The crates for transporting aircraft protected the planes during many days of rough ocean travel. The ends, top and sides of the crate did not touch the aircraft at any point. Following crating, these Brewster Buffalos (in a 1941 photo) leave Roosevelt Field for the waterfront to be loaded onto ships heading for Midway . . . and disaster. *(Photo: George Dade.)*

244

245

246

247

247. On average it cost $1,000 to prepare a warplane for export. Disassembly, preparation and crating entailed a considerable amount of work. This Grumman "Widgeon" is secured to the base of a rather large crate at Roosevelt Field. Grumman "Avenger" disassembly is taking place in the background. *(Photo: George Dade.)*

248. Vought "Kingfishers" for the Dutch being crated at Roosevelt Field, in 1939. Note the extensive use of waterproof paper sealed with tape to protect the aircraft from salt-air corrosion or saltwater spray during the crossing. Also note the four six-by-eight-inch fir stringers that run the full length of the crate as the foundation for a solid floor. *(Photo: George Dade.)*

249. A North American AT-6 being processed at Newark. Dade processed 50 aircraft per day on a moving disassembly line at their Newark facility. These mechanics are removing the cowling and propeller before spraying the engine and all exposed parts with an anticorrosion compound that was a variety of wax similar to weatherproofing auto polish. *(Photo: George Dade.)*

248

249

250

250. The 10,000th Republic P-47 built, and, by pre-arrangement, the 5,000th P-47 shipped by Dade, is here being inspected by General Farthing, Commander of the Newark Air Corps facilities. The waterproof paper protected the plane from any rain that penetrated the crate or water that flowed into the hold of the ship. *(Photo: George Dade.)*

251. Often, aircraft were prepared and crated right on the factory site and then shipped to the dockyards by rail. Here, in 1944, Waco CG-4A troop gliders are heading from Ford's Michigan plant for the West Coast. After the war these large wooden crates became popular with farmers, who bought them as surplus and used them for prefabricated buildings. The gliders inside were thrown away. *(Photo: George Dade.)*

252. Planes that were too large for crates were "deck processed" and shipped on the decks of freighters. The aircraft were sprayed with waterproof wax, covering every spot where corrosive salt air might penetrate. They were then wrapped with waterproof paper. These Grumman Avengers are leaving Roosevelt Field for the New York waterfront, in 1942. Late in the night, long lines of heavily loaded trucks with police escorts often rumbled over Long Island roads heading for the docks of Brooklyn, Jersey City or Hoboken. *(Photo: Grumman Corporation.)*

251

252

253

255

254

253. A Douglas A-20 "Havoc" receiving special treatment before being shipped on a freighter's deck. Following the protective spraying, the wings will be removed. This work is being performed at Dade's Newark facility. *(Photo: George Dade.)*

254. During the war, Dade developed a special plastic spray coating for aircraft not being crated. Called Eronel, the spray protected planes during the ocean crossing and was then peeled off at its destination. At Newark, these A-20's have just been coated, and are now being loaded on barges for shipment across the harbor and onto large freighters. *(Photo: George Dade.)*

255. A completed Curtiss P-40, now dismantled and being prepared for overseas shipment from Buffalo. The propeller, spinner and some engine cowling have been removed. Workers are now packing the engine with silica gel desiccant to absorb any moisture that might reach the engine during the long voyage. The fuselage has also been securely packed into a cradle that will serve as the base of the shipping crate. All large bombers, such as B-17's, B-24's and B-29's, were flown overseas directly to the front. *(Photo: National Air and Space Museum.)*

End of the Line

257

256. With the end of World War II, the age of the propeller-driven fighter and bomber was over. Postwar America had little need for thousands of B-24's and P-47's. Soon new types of jet fighters and bombers would sweep them from the skies. America's great aerial armada was gradually gathered up for destruction. Fields of aircraft, such as this one in the Arizona desert in 1946, began to appear as the warplanes were centralized for scrapping. These B-17's and B-24's would soon be unceremoniously cut up and melted down for their aluminum for postwar civilian products. *(Photo: Cradle of Aviation Museum.)*

257. After the war, great fleets of American warplanes, many of them hardly more than a year old, were parked to bake in the sun until the moment of their destruction. Many of these B-17's, now moldering in a field in Arkansas in 1946, are probably veterans of desperate combat in the skies over Europe. The miracle of their production would soon turn into the miracle of their rapid destruction. By three years after the end of the war, comparatively few World War II warplanes had survived, having been sold off to scrap dealers and quickly melted down. *(Photo: National Air and Space Museum.)*

258

258. A fighter's wing section is seen here being cut up and fed into a smelter's oven for its aluminum content. Wartime P-51's and B-24's would now evolve into postwar baby carriages, razor blades and pots and pans. In spite of the fact that America produced over 300,000 planes during World War II, comparatively few have survived. Four Grumman F4F's survive, about a dozen B-24's and two or three P-61's—but some types, such as the Brewster Buffalo, have vanished altogether. (See Appendix E.) This is a shame, because the massive production of aircraft by millions of American men and women during World War II was a phenomenon that will probably never be seen again . . . . *(Photo: Cradle of Aviation Museum.)*

Afterword

Where Are They Now?

Of the over 300,000 American-manufactured aircraft built for the U.S. and Allied armed forces during World War II, approximately 700 planes of combat type have survived to the present day, the vast majority having been scrapped for their aluminum content within several years of the end of the war. Propeller-driven fighters and bombers were replaced by much faster jet-powered aircraft in the late 1940's and early 1950's, and the survivors that were not scrapped were usually sent overseas to arm allied Third World countries. It was generally from these countries, especially those in Central and South America, that many of the currently flying warbirds were retrieved in the 1970's. Planes with nonmilitary uses, such as transports and trainers, have survived in much greater numbers.

The most common of the surviving transport planes is the C-47. These were used by the U.S. Air Force right through the Vietnam War and have since been sold off to small commercial operators. A lesser but still surprising number of Grumman Gooses still fly owing to their utility as small amphibious general-use planes in the Caribbean and Alaska. A great number of training aircraft still survive as well, types such as the PT-17, AT-6, BT-13 and L-4 having found continuing reliable use in pleasure flying.

Of combat types, a number of B-17's are still airworthy, and a handful are being rebuilt to fly. The B-17 has been employed in the U.S. as a fire bomber and in France as a survey plane, among other postwar roles. A large number of A-26's still exist, having served with the Air Force through the Korean War. Many were also later surplused out of their Arizona storage depot. Many Grumman Avengers are still flying, as the type was a popular fire bomber well into the early 1980's. When, after the War, an effort was made to supply Third World allies with former U.S. combat aircraft, in the 1960's and 70's countries in Central and South America became the recipients of B-25's, F4U's and P-47's. Without doubt more P-51's survive than any other combat type. P-51's were used by the USAF into the early 1950's (thus missing the great postwar scrapping), and then many were sold to Third World countries. Today, the cost of buying and operating a World War II aircraft has escalated far beyond what it would have cost originally. Unrestored combat types now sell for between $100,000 and $400,000; restored examples, between $400,000 and $1.5 million.

Currently, there is much controversy as to whether or not these surviving historic aircraft should be flown by wealthy individuals and "flying museums." Certainly it is exciting to see World War II combat aircraft in action. Yet each passing year brings increasing numbers of accidents and deaths resulting from flying these planes. These crashes are due to the extremely complex nature of these aircraft, combined with the demanding job of flying them. Sadly, not only do warbird crashes take lives, but each also results in the loss of yet one more historic aircraft. Ultimately, it will not be the lack of spare parts that grounds these aircraft, but rather legislation and/or prohibitive insurance. Fortunately, enough aviation museums exist around the country to ensure that examples of all surviving types will be preserved for future generations.

Glossary

Alclad: Aluminum alloy sheet with a pure aluminum coating to prevent corrosion.

Alloy: Usually, a mixture of two or more metals, or metal(s) and other substances. Alloys are usually stronger than pure metals or have other desirable characteristics.

Aluminum Alloy: A combination of aluminum and, usually, copper, magnesium, chromium and nickel.

Bulkhead: A circular framework conforming to the inside of the fuselage to give rigidity.

Cantilever: Said of a wing, rigidly supported at the fuselage, with the wingtip free to move vertically under the influence of vertically imposed loads.

Cowling: A removable streamlined metal covering that extends over and around the engine and sometimes over a portion of the fuselage as well.

Extrusion: The process by which aluminum and steel are shaped into intricate cross-sectional shapes by being forced through a die while hot.

Firewall: A fire-resistant bulkhead (here meaning a wall, as a ship's bulkhead) set to isolate the engine compartment from other parts of the structure and thus confine the fire to the engine compartment.

Flush-riveting: Riveting two pieces of metal together so that the rivet head is flush with the outside surface of the metal. Used on the outside of wings and fuselages where protruding rivets would cause drag.

Frame: The lateral members of a monocoque or semimonocoque structure that give form to and maintain the shape of the structure.

Hull: The portion of a flying boat that furnishes buoyancy when in contact with the surface of the water. Usually incorporates the functions of a float and a fuselage in one unit.

Jig: A rigid structure that holds components while they are being fabricated.

Longeron: A fore-and-aft member of the framing of an airplane fuselage, usually continuous across a number of points of support.

Monocoque: A fuselage construction that relies on the strength of the skin to carry the load and give rigidity. Usually the only reinforcement consists of vertical bulkheads formed of structural members.

Nacelle: An enclosure fastened to the wing for the purpose of fairing, or streamlining, an object larger than the boundaries of the wing—usually an engine.

Rib: A member of a wing structure, forming a chord, that is used to give the wing section its form and transmit the load from the outer surface to the spars.

Semimonocoque: An aircraft skin reinforced only by longerons and vertical bulkheads, but with no diagonal members.

Spar: A principal, transverse, member of the wing structure, usually of very heavy construction, attached to the fuselage at one end, spanning the wing, and supporting the ribs.

Spot-weld: A weld, made usually by electricity, that is done not in a continuous seam, but only in spots.

Stiffener: A strip or channel of metal added to a part to strengthen it.

Stressed skin: Skin that is not just a covering but is part of the aircraft's structure and is thus stressed to take part of the load.

Stringer: A rigid beam, usually running the length of the fuselage; used to give strength and rigidity.

Supercharger: A mechanical means of increasing the quantity of air and density of fuel entering the cylinders of an engine in order to obtain greater takeoff power or higher-altitude capability.

Appendix A

Aircraft Production, 1940-45
(Ranked by pounds of airframe delivered by individual plants.)

Rank	Manufacturer	Plant
1	Consolidated Vultee (Convair)	San Diego
2	Boeing	Seattle
3	Douglas	Long Beach
4	Ford	Willow Run
5	Martin	Baltimore
6	Lockheed	"B," Burbank
7	Curtiss	Buffalo
8	Lockheed	"A," Burbank
9	North American	Inglewood
10	Douglas	Santa Monica
11	Grumman	Bethpage
12	Consolidated Vultee (Convair)	Fort Worth
13	North American	Kansas City
14	Republic	Farmingdale
15	Douglas	Oklahoma City
16	North American	"A," Dallas
17	Bell	Buffalo
18	Boeing	Wichita
19	General Motors (Eastern Aircraft Div.)	Trenton

Rank	Manufacturer	Plant
20	Martin	Omaha
21	Douglas	Tulsa
22	Vought	Stratford
23	Curtiss	Columbus
24	Republic	Evansville
25	Douglas	El Segundo
26	North American	"B," Dallas
27	General Motors (Eastern Aircraft Div.)	Linden
28	Goodyear	Akron
29	Bell	Atlanta
30	Curtiss	St. Louis
31	Boeing	Renton
32	Douglas	Chicago
33	Brewster	Johnsville
34	Curtiss	Louisville
35	Brewster	Long Island City

Appendix B

Aircraft Production by Year

Year	Number of Planes
1940	6,019
1941	19,433
1942	47,836
1943	85,898
1944	96,318
1945	47,714
1946	1,669
Total, 1940-1946:	304,887

Appendix C

Aircraft Production by Manufacturer
(July 1940-August 1945)

Rank	Manufacturer	Number of Planes
1	North American	41,188
2	Consolidated Vultee (Convair)	30,903
3	Douglas	30,696
4	Curtiss	26,154
5	Lockheed	18,926
6	Boeing	18,381
7	Grumman	17,428
8	Republic	15,603
9	Bell	13,575
10	Martin	8,810
11	Vought	7,890
Total:		229,554

Appendix D

Production Pooling of Major Contracts

B-17: Boeing, Douglas, Lockheed
B-24: Consolidated Vultee (Convair), Douglas, Ford, North American
B-29: Boeing, Bell, Martin
CG-4: Waco, Ford, General Aircraft, Curtiss-Robertson
F4F: Grumman, General Motors
F4U: Vought, Brewster, Goodyear
P-38: Lockheed, Consolidated Vultee (Convair)
SB2C: Curtiss, Fairchild (Canada), Canadian Car & Foundry
TBF: Grumman, General Motors

Hamilton Standard Propellers: Hamilton Standard, Frigidaire, Nash, Remington-Rand
Pratt & Whitney Engines: Pratt & Whitney, Nash, Buick, Chevrolet, Ford, Jacobs, Continental
Wright Engines: Wright, Dodge, Studebaker, Continental

Appendix E

Surviving Combat Aircraft
(Numbers approximate and subject to change.)

Type	Flying	Static Display
A-20	4	6
A-26	48	26
B-17	7	17
B-24	2	11
B-25	30	40
B-26	3	7
B-29	2	22
CG-4	0	4
F4F	1	4
F4U	23	28
F6F	8	14
FM-2	12	13
P-38	10	13
P-39/63	19	28
P-40	16	31
P-47	8	27
P-51	86	52
P-61	1	2
PBM	0	1
PBY	31	11
SB2A	0	1
SB2C	1	5
SBD	3	9
TBF	0	5
TBM	40	16

Index

The numbers are caption numbers unless otherwise indicated.

Plane Types

Plane Names

Engine Types

Types of Other Devices